helping

helping

HOW TO OFFER, GIVE, AND RECEIVE HELP

Edgar H. Schein

BK

Berrett–Koehler Publishers, Inc.
San Francisco
a BK Business book

Copyright © 2009, 2011 by Edgar Schein

Berrett-Koehler Publishers, Inc.
235 Montgomery Street, Suite 650
San Francisco, CA 94104-2916
Tel: (415) 288-0260   Fax: (415) 362-2512   www.bkconnection.com

Ordering Information
Quantity sales. Special discounts are available on quantity purchases by corporations, associations, and others. For details, contact the Special Sales Department at the Berrett-Koehler address above.
Individual sales. Berrett-Koehler publications are available through most bookstores. They can also be ordered directly from Berrett-Koehler: Tel: (800) 929-2929; Fax: (802) 864-7626; www.bkconnection.com
Orders for college textbook/course adoption use. Please contact Berrett-Koehler: Tel: (800) 929-2929; Fax: (802) 864-7626.
Orders by U.S. trade bookstores and wholesalers. Please contact Ingram Publisher Services, Tel: (800) 509-4887; Fax: (800) 838-1149; E-mail: customer.service@ingrampublisherservices.com; or visit www.ingrampublisherservices.com/ordering for details about electronic ordering.

Berrett-Koehler and the BK logo are registered trademarks of Berrett-Koehler Publishers, Inc.

Printed in the United States of America

Berrett-Koehler books are printed on long-lasting acid-free paper. When it is available, we choose paper that has been manufactured by environmentally responsible processes. These may include using trees grown in sustainable forests, incorporating recycled paper, minimizing chlorine in bleaching, or recycling the energy produced at the paper mill.

Library of Congress Cataloging-in-Publication Data

Schein, Edgar H.
  Helping : how to offer, give, and receive help / Edgar H. Schein.
    p.   cm.
  Includes bibliographical references and index.
  ISBN 978-1-57675-863-2 (hardcover : alk. paper)
  ISBN 978-1-60509-856-2 (pbk. : alk. paper)
  1. Helping Behavior. I. Title.
  BF637.H4S34   2009
  158'.3—dc22   2008038458

First Edition

16 15 14 13 12   10 9 8 7 6 5 4 3

Project management and book design: BookMatters; copyediting: Tanya Grove; proofreading: Oriana Leckert; indexing: Leonard Rosenbaum; cover design: Richard Adelson.

To my late wife, Mary,
who taught me everything I know about helping

contents

preface

Helping is a fundamental human relationship: A mother feeds her infant, a lover, friend, or spouse helps to make something happen, a group member plays his or her role to help the group succeed, a therapist helps a patient, an organizational consultant or coach helps to improve individual, group, or organizational functioning. *Helping* is a basic relationship that moves things forward. We take helping so much for granted in our ordinary daily life that the word itself often comes up only when someone is said to have "not been helpful" in a situation where help was taken for granted. Yet, as common as helping is in our daily life, it is paradoxical that we know relatively little about the emotional dynamics of that relationship.

A great deal has been written about formal help of the sort that is provided by psychotherapists, social workers, and other human services professionals, but not much is understood about what goes on and what goes wrong when I try to help a friend and find myself rudely rebuffed. How is it possible that the person jumping in to save the drowning man ends up getting sued for dislocating the man's shoulder in the rescue attempt? Why do so many consulting reports to management end up in the circular file? Why do doctors complain about patients not taking the pills that have been prescribed?

We understand both intuitively and from experience that to provide formal help, there must be both a degree of *understanding* and a degree of *trust* between the helper and the "client," the general term I will use for the person or persons being helped. Understanding is needed for the helper to know when to offer help and what would be helpful if asked for help. Trust is needed for the client to reveal what is the real problem, to be able to accept what is offered, and to implement whatever resolution might come out of the conversation with the helper.

In books on therapy a great deal of attention is given to building that trust, but in the day-to-day routines of giving and receiving help, the question of how one builds it, how one knows it is there, and how one maintains it are not well understood. In particular, most of these helping situations occur quickly, without warning, and are time limited. When a spouse asks for help in picking a suit for tonight's crucial meeting with the boss, we do not sit down and engage in the kind of inquiry that a therapist might use in starting with a new patient. When we offer to walk a blind person across a busy intersection, we do not think about building a trusting relationship before we grab his or her arm and move forward. Yet even there, we sometimes find the blind person saying, "No thank you" and pushing off on his or her own, leaving us wondering whether we have offended or whether the blind person is taking unnecessary risks in rejecting our help. How would we know?

A general theory of helping can only be useful if it explains the difference between effective and ineffective help in *all* situations, including the simplest ones, such as offering directions to someone who asks for help on the street corner. To develop elements of such a theory requires us to analyze what any relationship involves and what trust really means.

We must begin with the proposition that all human relationships are about status positioning and what sociologists call "situational proprieties." It is human to want to be granted the status and position that we feel we deserve, no matter how high or low it might be, and we want to do what is situationally appropriate. We are either trying to get ahead or stay even, and we measure all interactions by how much we have lost or gained. A successful interaction, one that leaves us with a feeling of accomplishment, results when we have acted appropriately in terms of our goals. Ideally those goals involve some gain for everyone in the situation.

What distinguishes the helping situation is that we are consciously trying to help someone else to accomplish something. The helping relationship is one in which we invest time, emotions, ideas, and things; hence we expect a return, if only a thank you. When it works well, we both gain status. But alas, often it does not go well and we run the risk of losing status— not helping when help was needed, trying to help when help was not needed or wanted, giving the wrong kind of help, or not sustaining help when it is needed over a period of time.

In this book I analyze the dynamics of helping relationships, explain the importance of trust in helping relationships, illustrate what any would-be helper must do to ensure that help is actually provided, and what any recipient of help must do to facilitate the process. I have come to believe that the social and psychological dynamics of helping are the same whether we are talking about giving directions or coaching an organizational client or taking care of a sick spouse. I therefore use a broad range of examples that I have experienced in my own professional and personal life. I have been in therapy, have been coached in tennis, and in many other ways have received help. As a helper I have been a husband, a parent to three children, a grandparent to seven grandchildren, taught many classes, consulted with individual and organizational clients, and have taken care of my wife during her years with breast cancer. It is through seeing the similarities in these many different kinds of situations that we can begin to build a more general theory of helping.

Intellectual Roots
and How This Book Is Organized

I have written this book more in the style of an essay than an academic study. My training at Harvard's Department of Social Relations exposed me to a great deal of sociology and anthropology, and I have always felt that these two disciplines were underutilized in our social and psychological analyses of social phenomena. In particular, it is the Chicago School, which developed "symbolic interactionism," that is most pertinent to the analysis of helping. First formulated by Cooley (1922), Mead (1934), Hughes (1958), and Blumer (1971), it was brilliantly expanded upon in the work of Erving Goffman (1959, 1963, 1967), whose microanalyses of social behavior are enormously insightful. I worked closely with Goffman during my stint at the Walter Reed Institute of Research where he was a consultant from 1953 to 1956, and I continued to focus on this form of analysis in my collaborations with my sociological colleague John Van Maanen (1979).

A second and very powerful set of insights came from several decades of work with the National Training Labs (Bradford, 1974; Schein & Bennis, 1965), where I ran sensitivity groups and participated in the design of learning labs at Bethel, Maine. Apart from the personal learning in the groups, the influence of that generation of researchers in group dynamics and leadership was profound. I want to single out particularly Doug McGregor, Lee Bradford, Ken Benne, Ron and Gordon Lippitt,

Herbert Shepard, Warren Bennis, Jack Gibb, Chris Argyris, Edie and Charlie Seashore, and Dick Beckhard.

The exposure to this group and the workshops that we collectively evolved put the focus squarely on interpersonal processes. The process focus combined with symbolic interactionism helped me to develop my own consulting style, labeled "process consultation" (1969, 1999), and the insights derived from many consulting experiences led to the realization that helping was not only an important ingredient of what organizational consulting was all about, but was a core social process in its own right that needed analysis.

This book is an exercise in conceptualizing experiences with which we are all highly familiar. I have not tried to include all of the research that bears on helping, as this is not intended to be a scholarly treatise. Instead, what I am after is practical insight that might improve the reader's understanding and skill in helping. What the reader should realize is that most current analyses of helping, coaching, and consulting have focused on the psychological factors, such as temperament and personality. It is my view that as important as those factors are, the key to understanding a relationship such as helping is to look at it from a cultural and sociological view.

The humorist Stephen Potter (1950, 1951) used his thorough understanding of the social rules of interaction to write semi-seriously about how these rules can be taken advantage of if the protagonist wishes to gain status or put his counterpart down. Though the examples he cites in *Gamesmanship* and *One-upmanship* are clearly caricatures, they are almost always just minor variations of what we can observe going on around us all the time. And it is not accidental that these two titles have become common words in our daily life, reflecting the universality of status rituals on behalf of our social goals.

Helping is a special kind of relationship and one must therefore be mindful of its special characteristics. In that regard I have also been highly stimulated by the seminal writings of Ellen Langer, especially her book *Mindfulness* (1989) which explores internally what Goffman so effectively explores interpersonally.

My basic argument, that social life is partly economics and partly theater, of course rests on a long tradition of scholarship and philosophy. There are few cultural universals, but anthropologists agree that all societies are stratified and that all social behavior is reciprocal. My observations and assertions about the helping process are my own, but are built on those two sociological and anthropological premises. They are intended to enrich our understanding by taking a somewhat different view of social interaction and the role that helping plays in our daily life.

In chapter 1 I review the many forms of helping to illustrate how broad and deep the concept is. Chapter 2 shows how the language and imagery of economics and theater help us to understand some of the fundamentals of all human relationships. In chapter 3 these concepts are applied to the helping relationship and the argument is put forth that all such relationships are initially unbalanced and ambiguous. Chapter 4 describes three different kinds of helping roles and argues that helping relationships should always start with process consultation. How to begin the helping relationship with humble inquiry is the focus of chapter 5 and detailed examples are provided in chapter 6. In chapters 7 and 8 I show how this model of helping actually illuminates some of the essential aspects of teamwork, leadership, and organizational change management. Chapter 9 wraps up with some principles and tips for would-be helpers.

acknowledgments

I have given chapters of this book to many friends and colleagues. They were very helpful at all stages in validating or challenging some of the ideas I put forth. Special thanks go to Otto Scharmer, Lotte Bailyn, John Van Maanen, David Coghlan, Sue Lotz, Mary Jane Kornacki, and especially the reviewers from Berrett-Koehler who provided detailed feedback on the draft. Joan Gallos and Michael Arthur read over the finished draft and provided yet another layer of help, which enabled me to clarify several ideas further.

My wife passed away during the writing of this book, but the last six months of her final battle with breast cancer after a good twenty-five-year fight provided much food for thought about helping and caretaking. I thank her posthumously for the fifty-two wonderful years we had together and for providing the creative home atmosphere that always made my writing a pleasure rather than a chore.

Edgar H. Schein
Cambridge, MA.
September 15, 2008

1

What Is Help?

Helpful and Unhelpful Help

Helping is a complex phenomenon. There's helpful help and unhelpful help. This book is written to shed light on the difference between the two. In my career as a professor and sometimes consultant I often reflect on what is helpful and what is not, why some classes go well and others do not, why coaching and experiential learning are often more successful than formal lectures. When I am with organizational clients, why does it work better to focus on process rather than content, or how things are done rather than what is done? My goal in this book is to provide the reader with enough insight to be able to actually help when help is asked for or needed, and to be able to receive help when help is needed and offered. Neither is as easy as we often wish.

The other day, for example, a friend asked me for some advice on how to deal with a problem he was having with his wife. I offered a suggestion to which he replied huffily that not only had he already tried that and it didn't work, but he also implied that I was insensitive to have even made that suggestion. It reminded me of many other situations I have witnessed where help was asked for or offered but the result felt unsuccessful and uncomfortable.

Then I was reminded of a case of helpful help. Outside my house a woman in her car drove up and asked me, "How do I get to Massachusetts Ave.?" I asked her where she was headed and learned that she wanted to go to downtown Boston. I then pointed out that the road she was on led directly to downtown and she did not need Mass. Ave. She thanked me profusely for not sending her to the street she had asked for.

The most common version of unhelpful help that I have experienced as both helper and client concerns the computer. When I call the help line I often don't even understand the diagnostic questions that the helper asks me in order to determine what help I need. When my computer coach tells me the several steps I need to take to solve the problem, I don't know how to interrupt to say, "Wait, I don't understand the first step." On the other hand, another computer coach I hired asked me what my personal goals were in learning to use the computer, elicited my desire to use it primarily for writing, and then showed me all the programs and tools that would make writing easier. That felt great. Yet when my wife asks me for help with the computer, I routinely fall into the same trap of telling her what I would do, which turns out to be more than she can handle, and we both end up frustrated.

Friends, editors, consultants, teachers, and coaches have often made suggestions and proposals that were quite irrelevant to my problem at the time. Even when I ignored them as gently as I could, my sometimes self-appointed helpers reminded me in an irritated tone that they were only trying to be helpful, implying that I was wrong in some way not to have been able to accept the help.

I remember one of my children asking me for help with her math homework. I interrupted my work, did the problem for her, only to find her sulking off without a thank you. What had I done wrong? On another occasion a child asked for homework help and I said, "Let's talk. . . ." I discovered that she wanted to talk about some serious social problems at school that had nothing to do with homework. We had a good talk and both felt better.

Doctors, therapists, social workers, and coaches of all sorts have had the experience of the best-intended help going wrong somehow. As a consultant and career coach to managers in various kinds of organizations, I have often figured out solutions to problems that they posed, and only later discovered that either my advice did not work or the client could not or would not implement what I had suggested. I also remember in my own consulting how often it happened that when I intervened to point out some dysfunctional behavior in a group meeting, I was thanked for being very helpful, only to find that the behavior did not change one iota.

Help is, of course, not limited to the one-on-one situation. Group effort and teamwork often hinge on the degree to which members perform their roles properly in accomplishing the group's task. We do not typically think of an effective team as being a group of people who really know how to help each other in the performance of a task, yet that is precisely what good teamwork is—successful reciprocal help. It is interesting to note, however, that the word "help" is only used in relation to teamwork when it does *not* occur, as when one group member says to another, "What you did was not helpful" or "Why didn't you help more?"

Helping in a team context is most obvious in team sports, where the ability of one player to score is entirely dependent on the skill of others to pass or block. There are many football stories of successful runners taking their linemen out to dinner after a successful game in acknowledgment of their support. Failure to help in this regard becomes obvious when the quarterback is sacked or the runner is tackled behind the line.

Clearly, there is more to helping or being helped than meets the eye. This seemingly common and very necessary human process is, in fact, fraught with difficulty and often does not succeed. This book starts with the premise that help is an important but complicated human process. I examine what it really means to help or be helped; what psychological, social, and cultural traps are inherent in this process; and how one can avoid them. As the examples above show, help refers to many things other than the professional help we expect from doctors, lawyers, ministers and social workers. So what is it all about and how do we ensure that it works?

The Multiple Meanings of Help

Helping is a very broad concept ranging all the way from the knight in shining armor rescuing the maiden before she is eaten by the dragon to the consultant working with an organization to change its culture to meet new strategic objectives or to improve its performance. From a client perspective, help includes not only what we ask for, but also the spontaneous and generous behavior of others who recognize when we need help even if we have not asked for it.

Consider the many life situations in which helping of some sort is involved (see Table 1.1). It occurs all the time in both formal and informal situations, and many of the roles described in Table 1.1 are ones we are called on to play ourselves at various times in our lives. To go one step further, helping is intrinsic to

TABLE 1.1   The Many Forms of Help

The *stranger* giving the tourist directions

The *parent* doing the child's homework

The *spouse* advising on what to wear for the party

The *nurse* assisting a patient with the bedpan

The *friend* supplying a word that is on the tip of your tongue

The *guest* offering to clear and do the dishes

The *teacher* explaining a concept to a student

The *computer expert* walking you through steps to fix a computer problem

The *911-hotline operator* or *suicide hotline operator* advising someone in distress

The *child* showing a friend or parent how to use a new phone or video game

The *coach* showing the client how to improve some skill

The *operating-room nurse* handing the surgeon the right instrument just in time

The *blocker* creating a hole for the runner to run through

The *executive coach* advising a manager on how to handle subordinates

(continued)

all forms of organization and work, because, by definition, we organize because we cannot do the whole job ourselves. Hired help truly refers not only to servants and caretakers, but applies equally to all organizational employees hired to do a specific job that we cannot do ourselves. Fulfilling one's duties in a job is, therefore, also a routine way in which we help. Consider the tensions that arise between supervisors and subordinates when either the subordinate did not put forth the effort to complete the task or the boss did not provide the time or other resources

TABLE 1.1   The Many Forms of Help (continued)

The *improvisation team member* setting up his/her partner to deliver the punch line and get the laugh

The *counselor* assisting a laid-off worker to find a new job/career

The *boss* advising subordinates how to do their job better

The *assembly line worker* putting his or her part in on time so that the line can move on

The *caregiver* ministering to a sick person

The *lawyer* advising and instructing the client on how to manage a divorce

The *social worker* suggesting how a family can cope with an economic crisis

The *psychotherapist* working with the client to cope with behavior problems or emotional difficulties

The *minister* showing a parishioner how to cope with guilt, grief or anxiety

The *doctor* diagnosing a patient and providing a prescription

The *funeral director* helping the grieving family cope with death

The *consultant* trying to improve the functioning of an organization

---

to get the job done. Workers and their bosses have a sort of psychological contract based on what kind of help they can expect from each other.

To illustrate further the extensive nature of this concept, note how many different words we use that mean to help in some way (see Table 1.2). Is there anything that all of these helping processes have in common? Is there an underlying cultural meaning that both helpers and clients need to understand better to improve the quality of help offered, given, asked for,

TABLE 1.2   The Many Words for Helping

Assisting	Enabling	Offering
Aiding	Explaining	Prescribing
Advising	Facilitating	Recommending
Care giving	Giving	Showing
Catalyzing	Guiding	Steering
Coaching	Handing	Supplying
Consulting	Improving	Supporting
Counseling	Mentoring	Teaching
Doing for	Ministering	Telling

and received? With the various kinds of help that exist—physical help, emotional support, information, diagnostic insight, advice and recommendations—do they need to be distinguished? How are they similar or different?

Formal and Informal Help

In the routine of daily life, help is the action of one person that enables another person to solve a problem, to accomplish something, or to make something easier. The person being helped might or might not have been able to do it alone, but helping implies that the task was made easier somehow, or, in the extreme, that it was accomplished at all (as when we save a drowning person). Help is thus the process that underlies cooperation, collaboration, and many forms of altruistic behavior. I will call this category "informal" help. In all cultures, this form of help is institutionalized and taken for granted as a basis for civilized society. It probably has some biological genetic basis since we know that non-human species engage in this behavior as well. Helping is part of what we think of as manners, rules of civilized behavior, and ethical and moral behavior. Such helping occurs all the time in a routine fashion. Note also that a request or offer of help cannot be ignored—it has to be dealt with in some fashion or the social fabric is torn a little and the actors are embarrassed.

The next level of help can be thought of as "semi-formal," where we go to technicians of various sorts to get help with our houses, cars, computers, and audio-visual equipment. Here we require help in making something work, are less involved personally, and pay for the service or information. Many of our most frustrating experiences both as clients and helpers occur in this domain because of our expectation that things should be easy to use and our unwillingness to adapt to new languages and routines such as those required by computers.

"Formal" help is needed when we are in some kind of personal, health, or emotional difficulty and need medical, legal, or spiritual assistance from someone licensed to provide such assistance. We go to doctors, lawyers, priests, counselors, social workers, psychologists, and psychiatrists for individual attention. When in our managerial and organizational roles we have problems of governance and organizational performance, we go to consultants of various sorts. In these cases the help comes from professionals and is a more formal process that implies contracts, timetables, and the exchange of money or other valuables for services. Most analyses of help deal with this formal level, yet informal and semi-formal help are far more common and often have greater consequences if not given or received effectively.

We will consider whether the help that occurs in more formal situations is different from the day-to-day informal and semi-formal help. What do effective trained and licensed helpers do that makes them more or less successful, and what can we learn from them to enhance our skills in less formal settings? Equally relevant is to ask what the trained helper can learn from a closer examination of the dynamics of informal and semi-formal help.

Helping Is a Social Process

Helping involves more than one person, so I will concentrate on how to think about and define the helping *relationship*. That focus will, in turn, lead us to a discussion of what is involved in *any* relationship and what it means to have a *good* relationship, one in which we can trust each other and can communicate openly.

All relationships are governed by cultural rules that tell us how to behave in relation to each other so that social intercourse is safe and productive. We call this good manners, tact, or etiquette. Underneath this surface level of overt behavior lie powerful rules that must be followed for society to work at all. Some of these rules vary according to the situation, but in any given culture there will be a set of universal rules that, if violated, cause the person to be ostracized or isolated. When they are violated in an ongoing interaction we become offended, embarrassed, or suspicious that the relationship is not good. This may result in a lack of trust or hurt feelings if the client felt that no help was provided, or the helper felt refused or ignored.

Though helping is a relationship, the process of offering, giving, or receiving semi-formal or formal help usually starts with individual initiative. What we must understand, then, is how the initial contact between the potential helper and potential client evolves into a relationship that produces help. Someone

decides to give or offer help, and that action may lead to a helping relationship; or someone may ask for help, which could also
result in a helping relationship. A team leader brings together
a bunch of people and creates a relationship-building process
that leads to mutual helping among team members. A consultant helps a manager organize different units so that they can
help each other in achieving organizational tasks. Sometimes a
group or community recognizes that it collectively needs help,
but someone must articulate the need and bring it to public consciousness. A relational helping process can then be created.

The first thing to focus on, therefore, is how personal initiative leads to a relationship. If we understand the dynamics of
building any relationship, we can build a more effective helping
relationship.

In the next chapters I will examine what some of the ultimate rules are that govern relationships and how they apply to
helping relationships. We will examine the inequities and role
ambiguities of helping relationships, the different roles that
helpers can take once the relationship is balanced and comfortable, how to build such a relationship, and how to intervene as
the client/helper relationship evolves.

2

Economics and Theater
The Essence of Relationships

We learn early in life about two fundamental cultural principles. The first and most important of these is that all communication between two parties is a reciprocal process that must be, or at least must seem to be, fair and equitable. We must all learn the rules of social economics if we are to survive and be comfortable in the social world. At the simplest level, children learn they must say "thank you" when given something, or in some way acknowledge the gift. The thank you is the reciprocation, the giving back that closes the communication loop and makes that interaction fair and equitable. Similarly, children learn they must pay attention when spoken to. The word "pay" acknowledges that the other person has offered information or instruction of some value. As we will see, we expect reciprocation in all relationships. Failure to reciprocate risks offending someone and leads to a deterioration of the relationship.

The second fundamental cultural principle is that all relationships in human cultures are to a large degree based on scripted roles that we learn to play early in life and which become so automatic that we are often not even conscious of them. We must play our roles appropriately, and these roles must mesh in accordance with the given situation. When two people are talking they must decide who is actor (talking) and who is audience (listening). The roles can switch very quickly, but for social interaction to work, they must be complementary. The actual economic values involved in an interaction are defined by this second fundamental principle—the definition of the situation—which specifies the roles we are to play and the value we are to attach to them. If I signal by my voice and demeanor that I have something important to tell you, that defines the situation, the roles, and the exchange. You automatically take a more attentive stance and indicate through your behavior that you are listening carefully. You expect to hear something of importance and will be offended and irritated if I was merely trying to draw your attention away from what you were doing. I did not play the role properly according to the situation I had defined.

The normal process of daily life is a series of these definitions of the situation. They tell us what roles we should play and what to expect of others. For example, we learn that when a person of higher status appears on the scene, deference is required. When we get together with subordinates, circumstances dictate the proper demeanor consistent with our status. In this way we learn how to attach value to our own role and to the roles of others. Equity and fairness in the relationship does not mean equality of actual status, but behaving appropriately, considering the participants' relative status and the particular situation. The situation defines the amount of value that can be claimed by each participant. When I am introduced as a speaker at a big meeting I can claim more value and the audience reciprocates with more respect. If I meet members later over drinks, I still have higher status, but the circumstances now make it possible for me to be less formal, claim less value, and encourage others to address me more casually.

Colloquially, this value is what we call "face." In any given interaction each party claims a certain amount of face, and the rules of reciprocation require that the others in the situation confirm what is claimed, or give the person the face they demand. If I say, "I want to tell you something," I am claiming to know something that presumably will be of value to you. It is then your responsibility to listen attentively, not talk yourself, and pay attention. Again the word "pay" is used. Note also that we talk of investing in relationships and are, thereby, building social capital, which we can draw on later by asking for favors.

If we choose not to grant others what they claim by ignoring them or in some other way embarrassing them, they lose face and we show ourselves to be rude or aggressive. In that sense it is a cultural truism that when we fail to uphold someone else's claim, we both lose face. However, we may decide to politely accept a person's claims, yet, by clever words or demeanor, assert a higher status, thereby demanding that our own higher claim be granted. Social interaction is, therefore, either a delicate balancing act of mutual face maintenance or an opportunity to gain status, in what Stephen Potter calls "one-upmanship" (1951).

Situational roles and rules supersede even formal values that we espouse, as in the case where the child is taught never to lie, until the neighboring obese lady walks by, and learns not to call her a "fat lady." In fact, growing up is very much a process of knowing when to be frank, when to be diplomatic, and when to pretend that you did not see or hear something that might be difficult to respond to. It is this capacity to withhold or lie that creates issues around trust in relationships. Sincerity, congruence, and trustworthiness reflect the degree to which one is perceived to be consistent across various roles and how much one's public face matches one's inner values.

In daily life we, as functioning adults, have learned thousands of roles and scripts so that we can go smoothly through the process of identifying the various situations that we encounter or create, and manage the different relationships into which a typical day will plunge us. As we will see, these cultural dynamics are crucial in the helping situation because both client and helper enter the situation with a chosen amount of face. How the helping relationship evolves then depends on the degree to which the client grants value to the helper and the degree to which the helper grants value to the client; and in each case that depends on the amount of trust they have in each other. Let us examine these dynamics in greater detail.

Social Economics: Maintaining the Social Order

If all cultures are governed by the rules of equity and reciprocation that define how we value each other in our relationships, then what are the social currencies that are exchanged? They are love, attention, acknowledgment, acceptance, praise, and help. Help in the broadest sense is, in fact, one of the most important currencies that flow between members of society because help is one of the main ways of expressing love and other caring emotions that humans express. Informal help is so often taken for granted that we hardly notice it and rarely identify it as such. It is only when it is expected and not forthcoming that we identify its absence and react negatively to the person who failed to provide it. The implication is that if someone asks for assistance, we are obligated to provide it or have some acceptable excuse. Similarly, if someone offers help, the person to whom it is offered is obligated to accept it or have some excuse for not accepting it. A request requires a response and an offer obligates a thank you. To label a person as "not helpful" is clearly a negative statement and raises questions about that person's reliability as a member of the group.

The amount of value we attach to ourselves and to each other is conveyed through our social behavior, through the line we take and the face we project. The unwritten economic rules of how much we may claim and how much we must protect the face of the claimant will differ depending on the culture and circumstances, but our daily language illustrates very well the degree to which social interaction is an economic phenomenon.

Consider the economic language used in everyday interactions. You can pay attention, pay your respects, pay off social debts, pay a compliment, and pay the piper. Also part of our vocabulary is the concept of sales. You can sell yourself short, sell your point of view, be sold up the river, or ask sarcastically, "What's he selling today?" Of course, where there's selling, there is usually buying. You can buy good will, but you don't buy an unlikely story. There are many terms that point out the ways in which people give and take, and keep track of these transactions. You ask to be given your due or you may feel short-changed. You are owed the courtesy of a reply and feel cheated when there is no pay-off after all the time and effort you invested. Even if no money is exchanged, you may ask someone to lend an ear or borrow his strength. Metaphors concerning social interactions abound—an eye for an eye, a tooth for a tooth; don't get mad, get even; he got his just desserts; scratch my back and I'll scratch yours.

The degree to which these economic processes are embedded and ritualized can easily be seen in even trivial daily interactions. If we give something to a beggar and he does not acknowledge it, we feel cheated or unappreciated. To regain our sense of social equity we either psychologically claim more value for ourselves by saying to ourselves or a companion, "I was a generous person to have done that," or we reduce the value of the other person by declaring, "What an ungrateful wretch!" Until the situation is back in equilibrium we remain vaguely uncomfortable. We do not want to lose face; or to put it more generally, our self-esteem is based on continual acknowledgment through reciprocation that what we have claimed for ourselves has been accepted and confirmed. This could be done with a body posture that shows attentiveness or just a nod of the head that shows understanding.

This process of perpetual mutual reinforcement is the essence of society. What we call good manners or etiquette is, in fact, culturally necessary in daily life. We have all experienced the tension that arises when we are in a new culture and don't know the rules of mutual acknowledgment. When the rules are broken and not repaired we feel humiliated or offended. One who deliberately fails to maintain the other person's face causes humiliation, and is therefore regarded as someone who is offensive and should be avoided. In the extreme, when someone consistently breaks these social rules, we define them as "mentally ill" and incarcerate them. In other words, if we were to disregard these rules and stop acknowledging each other, social life would deteriorate rapidly into individualistic, competitive mob behavior and anxiety levels would skyrocket.

To experience how powerful these rules are, try the following social experiment. The next time a friend or spouse starts to tell you something, freeze your own behavior—don't nod, keep a deadpan, and don't say anything. Within five to ten seconds the other person will ask you if anything's the matter, if you're okay, if you're paying attention, or in some other way will indicate that you are doing something that is not accept-able. You have broken the social fabric and it must be put right by some explanation or apology like, "Oh, sorry, I was thinking of something else." That may or may not have been true, but the social rules require a legitimate excuse. It would not have been all right to respond, "I was not interested in what you had to say."

When social exchanges don't work properly because the two people involved define the situation differently and are, there-fore, using different currencies, the result is anxiety, tension, anger, discomfort, embarrassment, shame, and/or guilt. What was given and received is perceived by either or both parties to be inequitable: "I came to this counselor to get some help with my problem and he did all the talking, so I never got to tell what was really bothering me," or "I paid a lot of money expecting some advice and all the counselor did was listen and play back to me what I said—what kind of help is that?" When clients ignore advice or refuse to accept help that is offered, this can be equally upsetting. Resolution of such tensions often does not occur until one or both parties have discovered the inequity and have made amends with an explanation, an apology, or a belated thank you.

Intimacy and Trust

Even though the rules are clear enough, our personal prefer-ences come into play as to when and how to build relation-ships or avoid them. Most of us know and adhere to the basic rules of etiquette, but we still exercise choices and preferences. Thus a person with a high need for inclusion and/or sociability might be more likely to affirm whatever others present, while someone who wishes to dominate might consistently compete and play one-upmanship in all of his or her relationships, and someone who prefers autonomy might avoid helping situations altogether. But these variations occur within the boundaries of the cultural rules. More important is to recognize that our conscious or unconscious manipulation of these rules is the basic mechanism by which we build, deepen, and test relationships. In a distant impersonal relationship we can only claim a little value for ourselves. In an intimate friendship or spousal relationship we can claim a great deal of value for ourselves by revealing private thoughts and feelings that we expect to be heard and acknowledged. We build intimate relationships in part to create situations in which we can confirm and increase our sense of self-esteem because we can claim more value for ourselves and count on its being accepted and affirmed.

Sometimes we test a relationship by initially claiming a high value for ourselves to see whether the other person will respond appropriately. We do this by announcing a high status ("Hi, I'm Professor Schein from MIT ...") or by revealing something more personal and meaningful ("I really am not feeling too great today ..." or "I've just come from my therapist. ...") to see whether the other person will understand, respond with sympathy, and acknowledge what we have said. Often this acknowledgment occurs through the other person revealing something more personal as well. And it is through cycles of this kind of testing and response that we build what we eventually call a more intimate relationship.

Trusting another person means, in this context, that no matter what we choose to reveal about our thoughts, feelings, or intentions, the other person will not belittle us, make us look bad, or take advantage of what we have said in confidence. Notice how this works in ordinary conversation. If you do not pay attention, if you start a side conversation, if you look over the person's shoulder at someone else who is more interesting to you at that moment, if you yawn, if you interrupt with, "I already knew that," or use a disinterested tone of voice—these are all behaviors that would disrupt the building of that relationship, threaten the speaker's face, cause potential embarrassment, and lead the speaker to conclude that you are rude, or at least not worth relating to, and should be avoided in the future. On the other hand, if you pay attention and indicate your interest in other ways, you are then building the relationship and can make claims on it later when you want to tell something and expect the other to listen attentively.

We use our knowledge of the rules and our early experiences when we interact with other persons to select those relationships that we want to encourage or discourage. If conversations with some people are consistently inequitable, we don't build a relationship with them and learn to avoid them in order to escape such discomfort. If work or other circumstances require us to interact with such persons, culture provides yet other rules for how to be polite but formal. We have all learned how to send signals that we want to remain distant and formal, and we know how to send signals that we want to become closer. In either case, equity and fairness, consciously and unconsciously govern how we will feel in the relationship and how deep we want it to become.

The depth of a relationship can then be defined in terms of the amount of value we can safely claim for ourselves in what we reveal about ourselves. In this context, trust means safety for our self-esteem. In a deep relationship we make ourselves more vulnerable to being taken advantage of, to being ignored, to being belittled, or to not being acknowledged in other ways.

When a conversation has not been equitable we sometimes feel offended. That usually means that the value we have claimed for ourselves has not been acknowledged, that the other person or persons did not realize who we were or how important our communication was (as claimed by us). To avoid this from happening, we have to enter new relationships cautiously and with full consciousness that rules of reciprocity and equity have to be figured out and obeyed. The safest approach therefore is often the most formal, thus the need for such extreme formality in international diplomacy, since offense between countries cannot be risked. Formality protects both parties from feeling affronted. However, situational proprieties can change these rules. If I meet an old buddy and treat him very formally because I don't remember him, he could well take umbrage at being forgotten, and I could be quite embarrassed by my memory failure. If we offer help, we expect one of two things to happen. Either it is accepted and appropriately appreciated afterward; or it is not accepted, but we are thanked immediately for our offer. It is not OK for the other person to walk away without a response. If offered help, we either have to accept it and be grateful for it or refuse it right away with a polite thank you and/or an explanation of why we cannot accept it. In either case the offer must be dealt with. We all have learned how to judge, given a particular situation, what kind of response is appropriate and fair. Even if I don't think I need it, I may accept help from my boss in front of others because the occasion calls for it. However, when we meet at a local bar, my boss may signal that less formality would be appropriate, allowing me to casually refuse the help with just a thank you. To illustrate this further, in the Japanese culture, subordinates are expected to go out drinking with their boss so that they can give the boss and each other feedback by saying things that would offend and threaten face if they were said soberly and at the place of work.

In conclusion, trust has two components that derive from social economics. Trusting another person means that 1) whatever value I claim for myself in interactions with that person will be understood and accepted, and 2) the other person will not take advantage of me or use my revealed information to my disadvantage. In any given relationship, the level of intimacy will reflect the degree to which the parties have learned to trust each other as they each reveal more about themselves. This mutual process of testing continues until a level is reached where either or both parties realize that if they reveal more it might not be understood or accepted. If either party violates the second point and takes advantage of what has been revealed by embarrassing the other or profiting somehow from the knowledge, then trust is lost altogether and either the level of communication reverts to earlier superficial levels or the relationship ends.

For example, I have been in a friendship that was deepening around more personal revelations until one day I overheard my friend tell another person one of my stories in a most belittling manner. I could never recapture the level of intimacy that we had achieved up to that time. Similarly, a consulting company that was successfully helping a school with a major reorganization lost the contract because one of the teachers had overheard one consultant tell another one, "It's an interesting project, but the teachers here are pretty dim bulbs."

Social Theater

The social economics described above reflect the ongoing theater of life. It is theater because what defines a situation is the perceptions of the actors and audience of the roles appropriate to that situation. Role relationships come to be scripted early in life, and the normal process of living can be seen as playing out a set of scenes in which we act out appropriate behavior. Such acting reflects our learning of how much value to claim for ourselves and how to play both actor and audience appropriately in the daily flow of social interaction. The degree to which the metaphor of theater dominates our thinking can be illustrated by the language we use.

We use many words and phrases that imply that we are playing a part. You can feed someone a line, play your part well at a meeting, ask what someone's role is, not like the part you are expected to play at a party, or give a scenario. When we are far from the theater itself we still refer to a person giving quite a performance, or declare that no matter what the situation, you can count on him to perform. We claim we've heard that song before and recognize when someone is giving us a song-and-dance routine. The word "show" comes up frequently in many instances, whether someone is trying to be the star of the show, get this show on the road, make a show of expressing sympathy, put on a real showstopper of a presentation, or steal the show. We are also told to get our acts together and act our age, but we don't fall for someone's act or want to follow a tough act. Sometimes we are accused of not acting like ourselves. Even the word "scene" pops up in everyday language. You may feel like a change of scenery or set the scene for a meeting, but you don't want to make a scene or let someone else steal the scene. One may direct a meeting, feel upstaged, put on a good front, or always speak in a stage whisper. And consider the question: "I wonder what was going on backstage?"

The first and most critical role relationship is parent and child. Learning how to be subordinate, how to get things without authority or power, and, most important, how to give persons in authority what they need to make the relationship feel equitable, occurs early but has to be practiced throughout life. There will always be people above us. As we grow up, we also eventually learn how to deal with peers and with people below us. We become adults and parents ourselves. The sociologist Erving Goffman (1967) described these as the rules of "deference and demeanor." As children and subordinates we learn how to be appropriately deferent; as parents and bosses we learn what kind of demeanor is required of us to gain and maintain the respect of those below us. For example, subordinates are not supposed to interrupt a superior, but a superior is allowed to interrupt a subordinate. When a superior is talking you are supposed to pay attention by adopting the appropriate body posture, indicate interest, and nod your head to convey understanding. If you are the superior, your communication should be authoritative and clear so that you can earn the respect of subordinates.

When the cultural rules are ambiguous or misunderstood, tragic consequences occur, as when white South African managers in the gold mines punished workers for being insubordinate and untrustworthy because they were shifty-eyed and "never looked you in the eye." What the managers did not understand was that under the tribal rules with which the workers grew up, it was a cardinal rule not to look directly into the eyes of a superior because that was a clear act of disrespect.

The dress code for subordinates is generally allowed to be fairly informal, while the boss is usually supposed to be more formally dressed—in uniform, so to speak. But we also learn that a meeting with the boss requires more formal dress as a sign of respect. Learning when and how to show respect is, in fact, one of the most important areas of social learning. We also learn that the boss who dresses informally wants to reduce the formal status distance. If that is not accompanied by other behavior that is more egalitarian, it can produce strained relationships. Subordinates may feel that the boss might take advantage of the closeness in various ways. The furor over sexual harassment in the workplace has highlighted precisely this aspect of the rules of deference and demeanor. A pat on the fanny, a hug, or the telling of a dirty joke across gender and status boundaries often creates strong feelings of inequity and exploitation.

The higher the status, the more formal and prescribed the rules are of demeanor. For example, one non-obvious function of giving senior executives private bathrooms is to give them space to compose themselves before they meet others of lower status. It also reinforces the notion that with status goes social value, and the higher the value, the more sacred that person becomes. Now that executive is stereotyped as having super or non-human qualities—one would not expect to meet Superman in the employees' bathroom.

Not only is there more formality for those in positions of authority, but there are more rules for their behavior in public and in relationships. Children have broad latitude as to what is acceptable behavior; parents and bosses are much more constrained as to what is appropriate in many kinds of situations. We are often shocked when some dignitary is discovered in an informal situation to be swearing, acting silly, or in other ways being out of role.

Harris (1967) in his insightful book *I'm OK, You're OK* points out that by the time we have become adults, we have the choice of entering situations as a "child," an "adult," or a "parent" because we have learned how to perform each of these roles throughout life. We know how to be "childish," "authoritarian," or "act our age." How we make this choice in any given situation is often predicated on our preconception of who the other persons are, what their personality attributes are, and what the status differential will be between us. If the other person acts very parental by talking down to us, we may feel it is appropriate to act childish by being passive-aggressive, though we may discover that it would have been more effective for both of us to have approached the situation in an adult manner.

One may wonder whether helping—true deliberate helping—is optimally an adult-to-adult activity in that this relationship is equilibrated a priori, even though formal rank or status differences between adults may be present. When we help in either the parent or child role, we are already taking a superior or inferior position, which might distort the process in unknown ways. A parent assisting a child would usually be considered parenting rather than helping, and one may want to speculate on whether the parent acting in the adult role might produce a different and possibly even better outcome. Thus the parent responding to the child's "Help me with my homework" could say, "What is troubling you?" (the adult response) instead of, "Let me see it; here is the answer" (one version of the parental response). Following this line of reasoning, what do we call it when the child helps the parent? There are wonderful tales of children caring for aging relatives, but we tend to consider them as unusual rather than the sort of helping one would expect. We are likely to think of such children as acting in a very mature (adult) manner.

In general, if the helper acts parental, the client may feel patronized; if the helper takes on the role of the child, the client is confused and wonders if the roles need to be reversed. I have described these dynamics in general terms, ignoring for the moment cultural variations. An amusing example of cultural variation in situational proprieties was the discovery during a consulting project with a European subsidiary of Exxon: executives who had to travel to the U.S. carried two sets of clothes—formal dark suits for the New York headquarters; and jeans, boots, and informal shirts for the Texas headquarters. Visiting high-tech start-ups often creates the impression that these young companies have no formal rules of deference and demeanor; but in fact, they are just different. I remember one such company in which status was communicated by the number of times one could roll up one's shirtsleeves. Communication in these organizations often seems totally casual, yet newcomers have to learn what is and what is not permissible when talking to the engineers or software programmers, who have higher status.

Personality also plays a role in how we are predisposed to take our roles in given situations, especially with regard to dependency. For example, a dependent person might consider a relationship equitable in which others take leadership roles, while a counter-dependent person might consider it equitable only if his or her opposition was acknowledged and respected. The important thing is to know oneself—to know what one's predilections and preferences are, inasmuch as those will determine our sense of whether the evolving relationship is fair and equitable or not.

Finally, how the rules play out also will differ by what the societal function of a given relationship is in a particular situation. For example, we engage in many commercial activities in which our relationship to the other person—often a salesperson or clerk—is formal, impersonal, emotionally neutral, and very specific in terms of the main purpose of the interaction. Intimacy is not expected, but trust is an issue because we have so few interactional cues to judge the reliability of the other person. In retail, the opening "May I help you?" signals an attempt to make you dependent on the salesperson, who in fact is dependent upon your decision whether or not to buy. Most of us have experienced the early conversation with an auto salesman—it is often a kind of ritual dance to determine who will be dependent on whom. Effective salesmanship depends upon the seller finding some need or desire of the customer that can be fulfilled by the product being sold. In that sense the sale does become helpful and it is the salesperson's role to seduce the customer into the client role.

Another class of situations involves the person needing a haircut, manicure, massage, or other service that requires direct physical contact with the client. The client has a specific need and the helper role is clearly defined but limited. The relationship remains formal and emotionally aloof by mutual agreement because the helper is given access to the client's body without being in an intimate relationship with the client. If the service is satisfactory, a less formal relationship may develop with the service provider, as when we have a favorite haircutter or personal trainer.

If the client need is more personal and specific—as when we need the advice of a lawyer, doctor, financial analyst, minister, or therapist—the situation becomes more complex. Initially it is formal, but as one attributes to the helper a broader range of expertise, one makes oneself more vulnerable. Whereas in the sales or service relationship the client clearly has the higher status and power because he or she can walk out easily, in the client-initiated formal helping relationship, it is the helpers who have the higher status and power because of their expertise. It is for this reason that helpers in this category have not only more extensive training but also must be licensed and adhere to professional standards and ethics. Formally hired helpers are in a position to exploit and take advantage of the client and must, therefore, be limited both by formal rules and their own internal standards. As we will see, because of this status imbalance, clients will often try to maintain the illusion that they have equal or even higher status because they control the pay that the helpers get. They will deny their vulnerability in order to maintain face.

Conclusion and Implications

For society to work at all and the social order to sustain itself, informal mutual help is taken for granted. In all forms of relationships the rules of maintaining face apply and the rules of deference and demeanor guide the way we help each other through every day of our lives. When someone acts too aggressively or passively, or does something that is embarrassing, we move quickly to repair the situation with denial, apologies, and/or by distancing ourselves from the situation. What we must understand better is what happens when the normal flow is interrupted by someone explicitly asking for or offering help. We must then focus attention on the helping process itself. Subsequently we realize that different rules may apply in the various kinds of relationships that have been described, and we must ask whether there are common essential dynamics in any helping relationship. If trust is essential to help, what does it mean to trust someone such as a car salesman?

Building a relationship, any kind of relationship, requires sensitivity to the social economics and cultural rules of face work, to make sure that we are each getting something out of it and that it feels fair. In the daily drama of life we play our roles in such a way that our own face and the faces of others are preserved. In growing up we have learned how to handle a myriad of situations, each of which require us to take the appropriate actor and audience roles.

The social values that can be claimed in each of these situations are defined by the type of relationship and the tasks to be accomplished. We cannot expect the computer hotline helper to get involved in solving a personal problem, and should not be offended when he or she shows lack of interest in such problems. On the other hand, we can expect a friend to pay attention and be concerned when we ask to talk about a personal issue with which we need help. If that attention is not forthcoming, and no explanation is given, then we may well be offended and not seek help from that person on a future occasion.

The implication for would-be helpers is to become conscious of social economics and the social theater that we all live in, to think clearly about the helper role in the various situations in which they may find themselves, and to assess what sort of currency and what kinds of values must be managed to make the relationship fair and equitable.

Finally, we must all become aware that in the daily flow of life, helping is itself an important social currency that can cause disequilibrium when not handled properly. Knowing when and how to give help and when and how to receive it from others makes relationships both more productive and more pleasurable. Helping is, therefore, both a routine process of exchange that is at the basis of all social behavior and a special process that sometimes interrupts the normal flow and must be handled with particular sensitivity. In the next chapter we explore the special conditions that come into play when formal help is asked for, and the traps that arise for both helper and client from this request.

3

The Inequalities and Ambiguities
of the Helping Relationship

We turn now to the particular underlying dynamics of helping situations and the pitfalls of creating a helping relationship. In this chapter I explore the social inequities and role ambiguities that are exposed when someone asks for help or when help is offered. In a mature trusting relationship, in the daily flow of informal help, and in a well-organized functioning team, these dynamics are mostly hidden, and a great deal of help occurs smoothly and without much notice. Giving and receiving help has been learned from childhood, and reciprocation takes place automatically with nods of the head, thank you's, and other acknowledgments. The roles of giver and receiver are passed back and forth without fanfare as needed.

It is when the relationship or team hits a bump, when something unexpected or new comes up, or when there is no relationship to begin with, that the roles of helper or client become salient and the social economics come into play. This can happen without warning in informal situations when we may suddenly find ourselves in a client role—we may need directions, we may need someone to pick something up that we dropped when our hands are full, we may need someone to open a door for us, or we may need to cross into another lane and for an anonymous driver to let us in. As friends or spouses we may want advice or support for some issue that has come up. As team members we may encounter a new situation that requires recalibrating our roles. We may observe someone in need of help and offer it spontaneously, sometimes eliciting surprise and maybe even dismay on the part of the client-to-be. When this informal kind of helping occurs smoothly, we don't notice the underlying dynamics; but when it does not, we become confused and puzzled about the causes.

Such dynamics become most visible when we get into life situations that are disrupted. We may find ourselves facing a problem that requires the formal help of specialists endowed with licenses, expertise, and special equipment, or we may need semi-formal help in areas such as technology and aesthetic diversity. In the first category the helpers—doctors, lawyers, consultants, priests, social workers, and coaches—are members of helping professions. In the second category helpers are computer consultants, financial advisers, decorators, landscape architects, contractors, and even salesmen. In these instances the motivation to seek help is based either on something going wrong that needs to be fixed or discovering that we want to improve in order to achieve some goal. We first examine the issues of economics and roles in the formal and semi-formal situations, and then see how they apply to the informal daily routines of life as well.

The "One Downness" of Needing Help

Helping situations are intrinsically unbalanced and role-ambiguous. Emotionally and socially, when you ask for help you are putting yourself "one down." It is a temporary loss of status and self-esteem not to know what to do next or to be unable to do it. It is a loss of independence to have someone else advise you, heal you, minister to you, help you up, support you, even serve you. It never ceases to amaze me when I observe someone stumbling or falling down on the street how the first thing out of his or her mouth is invariably "I'm OK." Even when we are clearly hurt we are reluctant to accept the suddenly imposed state of dependency. At the extreme we feel humiliated, as when we need help with the bedpan in the hospital.

The need to feel in control is especially strong in those cultures in which growing up means becoming independent, and is especially strong for males in those cultures. Being independent means you do not to have to ask for help. Needing help often feels demeaning. In U.S. culture the quip is often heard, "Real men don't ask for directions, they figure it out for themselves." Seeing a psychotherapist for emotional problems is often viewed as something to be hidden. Bringing in a consultant means we can't solve our own problems. In these kinds of cultures, the U.S. being a prime example, the stigma of needing help also shows up in the reluctance to admit or advertise that one uses servants of various sorts.

The sense of being one down applies not only to one's perception of oneself vis-à-vis the helper, but can be even more strongly felt in relation to others in one's work organization. In many companies, to seek the help of a consultant is tantamount to admitting that one cannot do one's job. During my quarterly visits to a European company where I worked as a consultant for five years, I would occasionally be taken to lunch in the executive dining room. I would encounter there some of the individual executives with whom I had worked on various projects and would discover that they avoided my eyes and walked past me as if they did not know me. My host explained that clearly they did not want their colleagues to see that they had spent time with me because that would be a loss of status.

One can see the counterpart of this kind of feeling in the embarrassed looks that are sometimes exchanged between the patient leaving the psychiatrist's office and the others in the waiting room, leading some psychiatrists to provide the privacy of two doors—one to enter and one to exit. Given such cultural norms, the foremost problem is actually to ask for help, which puts the client one down and creates a status imbalance with the helper-to-be. The psychiatrist Irving Yalom (1990) captures the issue well:

> The project of psychiatric treatment is fraught with internal inconsistencies. When the therapist treats the patient, it is understood from the beginning that the treatment pair, the two who have formed a therapeutic alliance, are not equal or full allies; one is distressed and often bewildered, while the other is expected to use professional skills to disentangle and examine objectively issues that lie behind that distress and bewilderment. Furthermore, the patient pays the one who treats. The very word treat implies non-equality. To 'treat' someone as an equal implies an inequality which the therapist must overcome or conceal by behaving as though the other were an equal.

The "One Upness" of Being Asked to Help

Being thrust into the role of helper is immediately a gain in status and power—literally if I help someone up who has fallen, or symbolically if I am a counselor, consultant, or coach who is being asked to provide my wisdom and expertise to solve a problem. In terms of our face-work analysis, the person who asks for help is defining the situation as one in which power and value has been bestowed on the potential helper, whether or not that person can actually help. It is this bestowing of power that creates an imbalance in the relationship. After the help has been asked for, the client takes on the passive, dependent audience role and puts the helper-to-be into the actor role. The ball is suddenly in the helper's court—what will the helper do with it?

It is important to recognize this nuance because it provides the potential helper with the possibility of taking advantage of the situation—either selling something or in other ways exploiting the situation rather than providing help. One may realize that one cannot really help but be seduced into using the power granted for personal gain. It is psychologically hard to give up such granted power, to say with humility, "I don't know if I can help or not" or "I cannot really help you." There is a huge temptation to take a chance that one can help. I notice this especially if someone asks me for help with a computer problem. Even if I know that I probably don't understand the situation any better than the person asking, I leap in and try to help, sometimes making things worse.

Another complication is that being asked for help obligates one to respond. One has been put on stage. The door to a relationship has been opened and one cannot just walk away from the situation because providing help is culturally an important obligation to fellow members of the society. By asking for help, the potential client becomes vulnerable and creates a situation that requires rebalancing. For example, a colleague or friend seeks you out to get some advice on a personal matter: "Can I talk to you for a minute about something? I need some advice . . ." The cultural rules of social interaction require that you respond in some meaningful way. You either have to say, "Sure, let's sit down and talk . . ." or "I would love to, but can we do it later? I am in the middle of something . . ." Either of these responses acknowledges the client's need and equilibrates the situation by granting the person the status of having gotten your serious attention. That attention gives face.

What you cannot do without offending the person is to ignore the request or refuse to get involved. Such a response would reinforce the one-downness of the client by signaling that his or her problem is not even worthy of your attention. We sometimes feel this impact most in the more formal helping situation when a doctor or lawyer to whom we have gone for help turns us down, but it is just as painful when a friend or spouse indicates unwillingness to help, once we have asked. Note, by the way, that the professionals usually try to ameliorate the offense by acknowledging the validity of our claim and by offering to refer us to one of their colleagues. If they simply said no and dismissed us, we would feel bad indeed.

In summary, at the beginning, every helping relationship is in a state of imbalance. The client is one down and therefore vulnerable; the helper is one up and therefore powerful. Much of what goes wrong in the helping process is the failure to acknowledge this initial imbalance and deal with it. The reason the helping relationship has to be *built* rather than just being assumed is that, although the imbalance is clear, the social economics of how to fix it are not. Neither helper nor client initially knows what to expect and what to give to the relationship. In the case of professional help, actual money is involved; but in all forms of help, something of value is expected to be given by the client to the helper in exchange for the help. At the very minimum, after help has been given, the client is expected to be appreciative and to offer thanks.

The initial power imbalance—the implied dependency of the client on the helper and the ambiguity about what each should expect of the other—creates anxiety and tension in both that must be dealt with (Schein, 1999). The form that such anxiety will take varies with the nature of each relationship and the situation. In a formal meeting with a therapist or coach whose status has been touted by others ("Go to Mr. X, he'll be great."), we will be deferent and may be scared of what we are told or asked to do. If we take the same question or issue to a particular friend, we will worry that we are imposing, wonder whether we are overstepping the friendship boundaries, and hope that the friend will take us seriously and not belittle us or blow us off. In other words, once help has been asked for, anxiety is intrinsic to the situation, no matter what the initial relationship is between the client and would-be-helper.

If the existence of that anxiety is not recognized at the time, both parties are vulnerable to dysfunctional, defensive behavior. It is the immediate need to reduce that tension that leads to several possible emotional reactions that are normal but can easily bias the evolving relationship, which makes helping more difficult. These emotional reactions are potential traps into which either the helper or client can fall. These traps are most visible when someone is formally asking for help, but such reactions and consequent behaviors exist in all helping situations.

Let us look first at the five traps that exist for the client. I start with the client's emotional reactions because these are often not immediately perceived by the helper, yet need to be taken into account in choosing an initial response.

Five Possible Traps for the Client

1. *Initial mistrust.* Will the helper be willing and able to help? Such caution is normal and appropriate but may cause the client to hide the real problem at first. Instead, the cautious client may float some hypothetical dilemma to determine how responsive or sympathetic the helper will be.

"Dad, can you help me with this math problem?" asks a son who really wants to talk about some deeper personal concerns but does not know how to ask for time with his father.

"Doctor, I am having some sleep problems," says the patient who is actually having severe anxiety attacks during the night.

A manager says to a management consultant, "I would like you to help me with some team building for my group" when the problem is that the manager has lost faith in one of her subordinates but does not know how to deal with it.

The trap for the helper is to move too rapidly to solutions, to provide advice or guidance on the hypothetical problem and, thereby, cut off the opportunity to learn what the real problem might be. Working the hypothetical problem does little to equilibrate the relationship.

2. *Relief.* Having finally shared the problem with someone else who may be able to help, the client certainly feels relieved. Along with that often comes a welcome sense of dependency and subordination to the helper, which can become a trap if the solution to the problem requires effort from the client.

"I'm really glad to be able to share this problem. What should I do now?"

"It feels great to know that someone else might be able to help."

"It's wonderful that you understand what I'm going through."

Even if the immediate problem could be solved without the client's involvement, eventually the client will have to take charge of the situation. If the helper reinforces the dependency, it may be harder to get the client to become proactive later. Permanent dependency may be appropriate in some cases of caregiving, as when we push a relative in a wheelchair or pick things up for someone who cannot bend down. But in most helping situations, one of the goals is to enable the client to solve the problem if it recurs. In all those instances the relationship must allow and stimulate a gradual reduction of the client's dependency.

3. *Looking for attention, reassurance and/or validation instead of help.* Helpers have to be particularly sensitive to persons who ask for help but who really want something entirely different. Not everyone who asks for help is actually seeking it, but "help" may be a convenient word for whatever is being sought. Since it is not socially appropriate to say, "Pay attention to me," we can force someone to give us attention by asking for help because that request imposes an obligation to respond. Sometimes the potential client has already defined the problem and worked out a solution, but wants confirmation, positive evaluation, maybe even praise. This often happens in organizations where the consultant is hired to develop a program only to discover that the client already has one and wants the consultant to bless it.

"We have had this problem and I'm very proud of how we have handled it. Don't you agree?"

"What I'm planning is _____. Isn't this the right course to pursue?"

"I would like you to evaluate what I have done here."

The main danger in this situation is that the client has chosen this presentation to avoid feeling "one down" and has concealed the real problem that requires help. The helper must then find a way of reassuring the client without giving tacit approval to a solution that may not be relevant to the real situation. Secondly, the helper may approve the solution being mentioned when it is not really the way to solve the problem that prompted it. If the helper senses that this is not the answer, or that the wrong problem is being addressed, the issue must be reopened. If that does not work, it becomes necessary to withdraw from the situation with an apology.

4. *Resentment and defensiveness.* The client may look for opportunities to make the helper look inept. This reaction is most likely if the helper has already fallen into the trap of giving premature or irrelevant guidance, which may lead the client to belittle the advice, point out how immaterial it is, note that it has already been tried and did not work, or in other ways pull the helper down to regain a sense of parity.

"Your idea isn't doable because of _____."

"I've already thought of that and it won't work."

"You don't really understand. The situation is *much* more complex."

The trouble with this evolving relationship is that the equilibrium is gained by pulling the helper down instead of building the client up. The corollary trap for the helper, as we will see, is to get defensive and argumentative.

5. *Stereotyping, unrealistic expectations, and transference of perceptions.* Everyone has past experiences with helpers, which color their feelings and perceptions. It is intrinsically difficult to see a here-and-now new helper in a neutral way, but these biases are initially hidden, so the helper can only infer them as the relationship evolves. The client's projections onto the helper are sometimes based on deeper and unconscious feelings that initially neither the helper nor the client may be aware of. The helper may be perceived as a friendly or unfriendly parent, or resemble a loved or hated teacher from the past, and so on.

The potential problem is that the client then calibrates everything the helper does against these expectations and judges the quality of the growing relationship on this basis rather than on the help given. If past helpers have always been supportive and sympathetic, for example, the client may not be able to handle someone who just says "tell me more" or "what have you done about this?" instead of "you poor person, how unfortunate to have this problem." Given our human tendency to perceive the present in terms of the past, a helper might well ask early in the relationship whether and how the client had been helped in the past, which would provide valuable information for calibrating the present.

In summary, needing help and having to ask for it creates an uncomfortable and anxious situation that will produce emotional responses. A helper unaware of these responses may react inappropriately and make it harder to build a balanced relationship in which roles are clear.

Six Possible Traps for the Helper

A person who is asked for help or perceives that help is needed will automatically be one up, and there will be a strong seductive emotional force operating to take advantage of this position with a variety of reactions. Any of these responses can be normal and appropriate to a given situation, but helpers and clients have to be aware that since such reactions are a product of the helper being initially one up, they can also be traps that can create problems in the relationship. All of the six behavioral and emotional reactions I describe below derive from this feeling of being one up, of having some wisdom that someone else needs and wants.

1. *Dispensing wisdom prematurely.* Giving advice too soon puts the client even further down. This response also implies that

the helper assumes the problem presented is indeed the real problem, ignoring the possibility that the client is just testing the helper by floating a substitute.

"Ok, I've got it . . . Here is what you should do . . ."

"Simple, just do the following things . . ."

"Let me tell you what I did in a situation just like that."

In formal and semi-formal helping situations we are usually aware that we should take some time to find out what is truly going on if we want to be helpful. It is in the *informal* situation with friends, spouses, and strangers that we are most likely to fall into this trap by leaping in with advice before we know what is really being asked for.

2. *Meeting defensiveness with more pressure.* The helper often assumes that the client has revealed the actual problem and has the skills and abilities to follow through with the offered solution. Once the helper has fallen into this trap, it is very tempting to try to convince the client that whatever advice or recommendation has been given is likely to be correct and, therefore, needs to be argued and explained until it is understood. Helpers have found out, to their dismay, that this can be a path of destruction to the relationship because it frustrates both client and helper.

"I don't think you understood my suggestion; let me explain again."

"I understand your reluctance, but this is why my suggestion will work . . ."

"You aren't hearing me. Trust me. Try it out."

Once this response has been given, it is harder to back off because it will feel like a loss of face to the helper, who will then reason that the client is indeed incapable of understanding, doesn't really want help, or does not deserve to have more energy invested in the relationship. The most common version of this is when management consultants give their recommendations, find that they are not implemented, and try to convince clients to rethink their positions. If unsuccessful, they walk away with negative thoughts about the client. It never occurs to them that they may have been working the wrong problem or may have failed to build an equitable helping relationship at the outset.

3. *Accepting the problem and over-reacting to the dependence.* When someone rapidly agrees to take on the helper role and exudes confidence, it encourages the client to be dependent before really knowing whether the helper will be of assistance.

"I hear you and I can indeed help you. Let's get to work . . ."

"I understand your problem and I think we can do this together . . ."

"I can help you, if you can do the following things . . ."

On the surface these responses sound entirely appropriate, but they are likely to be traps because the helper cannot possibly know so early in the relationship that help can be provided, and it asserts unilaterally the superior position of the helper in the relationship. Reinforcing initial dependency can be dysfunctional because many kinds of problems require the active participation of the client in developing a solution. Here again, it is when working with groups and organizations that consultants or facilitators fall into the trap of taking over, not only making recommendations, but actually dictating next steps before knowing enough about what is possible, emotionally and/or culturally.

4. *Giving support and reassurance.* Sometimes it may be inappropriate to give support and may reinforce the client's subordinate status.

"You poor guy; I really feel sorry for you. That's a tough situation."

"Do whatever makes sense to you. I'm with you."

"I'm sure your plan will work, but if it doesn't, it won't be your fault."

There is a delicate balance between rationally assessing the situation and being supportive no matter what the client says. Automatic support can be a trap because it 1) puts the helper into the power role of expert diagnostician, 2) reinforces the client's subordinate status, and 3) could in fact be inappropriate since at that stage in the relationship the client may not be entirely forthcoming.

This trap is very common in organizational consulting because the client sees the problem as issues within the group itself and states it as such. This often masks the real problem, which is the relationship between that client and the group. Once the helper has expressed sympathy, it is difficult to get clients back on the hook to own the very problem that they may have created.

5. *Resisting taking on the helper role.* This response is the most subtle because helpers are often not aware that their efforts to be objective and avoid the above traps lead them into being so emotionally aloof that they convey an unwillingness to get involved at all. Emotional distance is often thought to be appropriate where formal professional help is sought because it reinforces the image of the objectivity of the helper. When that same aloof demeanor is demonstrated in informal situations, such as among friends, the message conveyed may be "I don't really want to get involved in your problem." The helper's dilemma then is to find the right mix of objectivity and

involvement so that if help is truly needed, the relationship can be built.

"Well, I don't really know how to help."

"I don't know . . . you might try the following . . ."

"Could we speak about this some other time?"

"Have you talked this over with _____? He might be able to help."

Why might such indifference occur? The most likely reason, psychologically, is that the helper realizes, consciously or not, that inquiring deeper into what the client may be feeling and experiencing may require a change in perception, which could result in giving up the power position and being one up. Becoming a helper often means that you have to allow yourself to be influenced, which may alter the way you see the situation. And, in fact, this willingness to be influenced—to listen to what the client is really saying and give up preconceptions of what the problem might be—is one of the most effective ways of equilibrating the relationship.

By genuinely listening to the client, the helper is giving the client status and importance and is conveying the message that the client's own analysis of the situation is worthwhile. If help is considered to be some form of influence, then the principle that you can only influence someone else if you are willing to be influenced yourself is quite appropriate.

6. *Stereotyping, a priori expectations, "counter-transference," and projections.* The helper is subject to all of these based on previous experiences. The client may resemble a person in a past relationship, leading the helper unconsciously to treat the present client in the same manner as an earlier one. Psychotherapists talk with feeling about the difficulty of treating a patient who

stimulates dislike or even disgust. The issue then becomes whether the helper is willing to expend the time and energy to find out whether the initial reaction, positive or negative, is realistic and how it might ultimately affect the possibility of providing help.

A particular version of this problem that I have experienced many times involves my own reactions to dependence or counter-dependence. I have found over the years that I relate better to a client who is independent or counter-dependent, and have difficulty listening to and responding to one who is very dependent. When the client slumps down, relieved to have revealed the problem, and says, "What should I do now?" I find myself getting anxious and maybe even a little angry. If I respond with "Well what are some alternatives that *you* can think of?" or "What have you tried so far?" and the client has some answers, then we can proceed. If, however, the client continues with "Oh, I don't know, tell me what I should do . . ." I find myself getting more distant, leading ultimately to suggesting that I cannot really help.

Helpers must be aware of their own emotional make-up and must be prepared to recognize that certain kinds of helper/client relationships may not be possible. In the more informal situation, the equivalent response to "Help me figure out which outfit to wear tomorrow," coming from a chronically over-dependent spouse, might simply be "You decide." That may settle the immediate situation but runs the risk that behind the inquiry there was a real problem that should have been addressed.

One way out of this dilemma is to say to the dependent client, "I am not sure I can help because I really feel that you should be more active in finding a solution yourself" or "I am uncomfortable telling you what you should do because I am not in your shoes and, therefore, can only tell you what I would do and that might not be at all appropriate."

Implications for Building the Helping Relationship

Building the helping relationship means to be aware of, avoid, or remedy the consequences of the traps that have been identified. What this implies is that the focus of the earliest interactions between the client and helper must be managed by the helper toward building up the client's status and identifying appropriate roles. This is not easy to do because the helper enters the relationship with a lot of psychological predispositions and cultural stereotypes. Just being asked for help is a tremendously empowering situation in that it implies that the client endows one with the capacity to help, with expert knowledge, with a sense of responsibility not to take advantage of the situation, and with the ability to deliver something of value.

What complicates the situation further is that helpers often feel frustration because they perceive themselves to be capable of giving so much more than the client seems to want, leading to disappointment when the help they feel they have given is not accepted as helpful. Professional helpers often feel frustrated that they are available but no one comes to them for help, a common situation for consultants inside organizations. When someone finally comes, there is so much relief that one risks overworking the situation and providing much more help than may be needed or wanted. I have a housekeeper who is very knowledgeable about homeopathic remedies and insists on suggesting the types of foods I should be eating. What makes this non-helpful is that she accompanies each suggestion with long, elaborate explanations of why this is the right food, to the point where I have to avoid her to save myself from twenty-minute lectures.

Helpers often perceive what may appear to be solutions far earlier than the client, or, worse, come to feel that the client is really stupid, messing up, not seeing the obvious, or not getting the message, which results in impatience, anger, and disdain. It is both puzzling and frustrating that what you regard as your most brilliant insight, advice, or intervention is hardly noticed, while some of your most routine questions or observations turn out to be crucial interventions highly touted by the client as being the most helpful. With all of one's theories and models of how to be helpful, it often seems that fortuitous events make far more difference than carefully calculated interventions.

Summary

At the very beginning of any helping situation, the relationship is unbalanced, which creates the potential for both client and helper to fall into traps derived from that imbalance. To build a successful helping relationship therefore requires interventions on the part of the helper that build up the client's status. In considering how to do this, the helper must first clarify what role to take vis-à-vis the client. What is often not evident is that the helper has a choice of role, and the way that choice is made has long-range consequences for the relationship, as the next chapter will explore.

Helping as Theater
Three Kinds of Helping Roles

At the beginning of any helping situation the appropriate roles and the rules of equity are inherently ambiguous, which means that both the helper and the client have to develop an identity and choose a part to play. This ambiguity exists even when the formal roles seem clear—as when we visit a doctor or go to a computer consultant—because at the outset neither helper nor client know all the facts. This mutual ignorance is rarely acknowledged explicitly, yet disregarding it is the reason for falling into the many traps outlined in the previous chapter.

The only thing that is clear when help is asked for or offered is that initially the client is one down and the helper is one up and, though they may not consciously feel it, both parties are anxious about how the situation will work out. If they are to form a successful helping relationship, they must deal with that imbalance by accessing their areas of ignorance and gradually removing them (Schein, 1999).

The number of things we don't know at the beginning of

a potential helping relationship is vast, but the information needed can be gathered very rapidly, even in the first few minutes, if we are conscious of the need and if we say or do the right things at the outset. I find that even in the simplest helping situations, such as being asked for directions, it is useful to take a moment to think about what I don't know and what the client does not know. Once we understand these areas of ignorance, we can select the appropriate roles to deal with them.

Five Things the Helper Does Not Know at the Beginning

1. *Will the client understand the information, advice, or questions being asked?* For example, when giving driving directions in Boston can you assume that the client knows what Mass. Ave., a traffic circle, and the MIT Bridge are? The computer consultant does not know if the client is familiar with a cursor or an icon. The automated telephone instructions do not consider that some people don't understand what it means to "hit the pound sign." The doctor may not be aware of the patient's pattern of food consumption when the prescription is to take the medicine "with meals." The organizational consultant does not know whether the client grasps the meaning of the word "involve" when asking the manager if the subordinates could become more involved in decisions.

2. *Will the client have the knowledge and skill necessary to follow the helper's recommendation?* For example, when the tennis coach instructs, "Bend your knees more," can the client actually do that? When the doctor says, "Relax," is the patient able to comply? When the organizational consultant asks a manager whether communications to colleagues and subordinates were

clear, there is no way of knowing whether that manager has the necessary skills to be clear.

3. *What is the client's real motivation?* When a wife asks her husband, "Do you like me in this dress?" is she really asking, "Do you still like *me*?" When a patient comes to the urologist to discuss urinary frequency, is it actually a request to discuss erectile dysfunction? For organizational consultants, this is their biggest area of ignorance, especially when the contact client wants them to work in some other part of the organization to diagnose what is wrong there.

4. *What is the client's contextual situation?* The helper does not know enough about the client's other relationships, group memberships, and cultural constraints. For example, we frequently train people in organizations to communicate and supervise in new ways, only to discover that the successful trainee reverts to the old style because the norms of the work culture do not support the new one. Similarly, the family therapist who advocates some new behavior finds that the client will not do it because of family norms. The financial adviser finds that the client cannot change spending habits because of some deep personality traits.

5. *How do clients' experiences shape expectations, stereotypes, and fears?* This is especially a problem in professional helping situations because potential clients have a wealth of invisible preconceptions of what therapy or counseling will involve, which may lead to high levels of anxiety and initial defensiveness.

So, the helping situation is not only full of the traps previously discussed, but is also very ambiguous. The first interventions of the helper must therefore be geared not only to ensure that the client gains status, but also to get crucial information about the client.

Five Things the Client Does Not Know
at the Beginning

The client approaches the helping situation with just as many areas of ignorance. A client needing help can get some relevant information before asking, especially in the formal help situation where helpers are often located through referrals. But a client who is suddenly offered help must find ways of removing these areas of ignorance.

1. *Does the helper have the knowledge, skill, and motivation to help?* Consider the times you have gone into a convenience store at a gas station for directions only to discover that the person at the counter either did not speak English or was new in town and did not know the street you were asking about. How often have we been left high and dry by potential helpers telling us they are too busy, can't help, or respond with "maybe later"? In the more formal situation, the therapist, coach, or lawyer knows that a request requires a response, so would either deal with it or refer the person to someone else, thereby saving face. The potential client must resolve this issue before investing too much time or energy in a relationship that may not provide help.

2. *What consequences will result from asking this person for help?* Have you had someone whom you asked for directions offer not only to tell you, but to actually show you, start walking with you, take your arm, etc.? My computer consultant would typically respond to a straightforward information question with a detailed and lengthy explanation of how the computer worked before answering the question. He would then follow up with several drills that he considered necessary for me to avoid asking the same question in the future. I often felt ambivalent about all the extra help I was getting that I had not asked for

and could not absorb. Clients know their limits and must try to get information about the level of involvement that will be demanded before entering deeply into the relationship.

3. *Can the client trust the helper not to use the situation to sell something or exert control inappropriately?* Most good sales efforts begin by doing something for the potential customer. If the salesperson does something for you, then you feel obligated in some way and are more likely to buy something. How often do you purposely not ask for help in order to avoid this potential obligation, or ask about something other than what really concerns you in order to test the other person? In the professional situation clients subjectively measure progress as the relationship evolves, and it can be very disillusioning to discover after several sessions that the therapist, coach, or management consultant is actually selling something.

4. *As the client, will I be able to do what is suggested?* I have never known what to do when my helper tells me more than I want to know or can remember, especially with directions or computer instructions. Do I ask for the information to be repeated, or write it down, which takes up more time? Do I request to see a map when I cannot understand directions? How do I respond to well-meaning help that is beyond my capacity to comprehend or implement, and what do I do then?

My son-in-law was teaching me how to use my new phone, so he held it in his hand and hit "menu," scrolled down to "addresses" (which was one of eight choices), hit the center black bar, looked at the list of items which came up, found the one I was looking for by name, hit the green bar, and the call was made. There were only two problems. One, I did not want to make the call; I wanted to get the number to write down. So I got the name, but still don't know how to get the number. Two,

I did not get a chance to practice the first two steps, so I have already forgotten how to access the menu and addresses.

5. *What will it cost financially, emotionally and socially to accept the help?* When a stranger has walked me to my destination or carried something for me, how do I reciprocate? When a friend has really helped with an important personal problem, how do I return the favor? The obligation that a client takes on is well illustrated in various stories that show dramatically how help and favors accepted at one point in time sometimes have to be repaid at a later time, even when it may not be convenient. As many Mafia stories illustrate, such accrued debts are especially common when the helper is in a position of authority. In formal helping situations paying for help somewhat reduces the ambiguity and minimizes the social debt that may be accrued.

The dilemma for the helper-to-be is now clear. Helpers not only have their own areas of ignorance, but must also be aware that the clients may be struggling with areas of ignorance as well. The helper's challenge is to choose a role which will facilitate the flow of relevant information.

Choosing a Role

There are three fundamentally different ways for the helper to respond immediately after being asked for help. These generic helping roles rest on different assumptions and have different consequences for the relationship (Schein, 1999). Even when the formal relationship specifies what kind of help is needed, as when we go to a lawyer or doctor, the helper chooses how to play the helper role at the beginning of the relationship. It cannot be emphasized enough that these are roles, not occupations. All of us are capable of playing each role, and we shift roles constantly as the situation demands.

The helper can choose to be:

1. An expert resource who provides information or services
2. A doctor who diagnoses and prescribes
3. A process consultant who focuses on building an equitable relationship and clarifies what kind of help is needed

The first two roles, the expert and the doctor, overlap to some degree and are very familiar. In fact, the cultural stereotype of helping is to be an expert or doctor. We have, in a sense, over-learned how to play these roles and we automatically attach high value to them, especially in the Western world. The process consultant role is more implicit and vague. It focuses initially on the interpersonal process involved in giving and receiving help instead of the content or problem that requires help. The focus on process is also something we learn early as an essential part of making any relationship more trusting and intimate. We learn that accepting each other at face value is an essential process to maintain and deepen relationships. What we often don't realize is that to build trust, we must apply these same process skills to all helping situations, especially with friends and spouses, where the situation is likely to be charged with emotions. In other words, just by growing up in this society we have all learned how to play each of these roles. But once we examine the assumptions that accompany each role, we see that it is essential to be in the process consultant role at the outset in order to access and remove some of the many areas of ignorance.

ROLE 1. The Expert Resource Role:
Provide Information or Service

This role is probably the most commonly accepted version of what it means to help. It assumes that clients seek from helpers some information or expert service that they are unable to provide for themselves. This can range from simple issues such as asking for directions to requiring help on complex organizational issues where managers are willing to pay a consultant. It would also cover those situations where we go to a supposed expert to get some advice on a personal problem. The essence of this role is that the helper's power rests on a body of presumed knowledge and skill that can be applied to the client's problem to make the situation better.

Organizational or management consulting often begins with the helper being recruited into this role. The client—usually an individual manager or representative of some group in the organization—defines a need and concludes that the organization has neither the resources nor the time to fulfill it. Then a consultant is sought to provide the information or the service and is paid for it. For example, a manager may wish to know how particular consumers feel, how a group of employees will react to a new personnel policy, or the state of morale in a given department. Then a consultant is hired to conduct surveys, either by interviews or questionnaires, and analyze the data.

The likelihood that this role will actually provide help depends on the following:

1. Whether or not the client has correctly diagnosed the problem

2. Whether or not the client has clearly communicated this to the helper

3. Whether or not the client has accurately assessed the capabilities of the helper to provide the information or the service

4. Whether or not the client has thought through the consequences of having the helper gather such information and/or implementing the recommended changes

5. Whether or not there is an external reality that can be objectively studied and turned into information the client can use

This role works well when the above assumptions can be met, and the areas of ignorance have been removed. We get all kinds of help from repair people, pharmacists, financial advisers, and experts of various sorts when we know what we need and have correctly estimated what the helper can provide. Informal and semi-formal helping situations can lend themselves easily to this form of help. But even in these situations, things can go terribly wrong because several of the above assumptions cannot be met, making it more likely that either the helper or the client will fall into one or more of the traps identified in the previous chapter.

Helpers who adopt this role from the beginning are less successful in situations where the problems are more complex. The frequent dissatisfaction with organizational or management consultants and the low rate of implementation of their recommendations can easily be explained when one considers how many of the above assumptions would have to be met for the information/service giver role to work effectively in complex organizational situations.

It should also be noted that in this process the client initially gives away even more power. The helper is commissioned or empowered to seek out and provide relevant information or expertise on behalf of the client; but once the assignment has been given, the client becomes dependent on what the helper comes up with. Expert helpers are also likely to provide only whatever they are good at—when you have a hammer, the whole world looks like a bunch of nails. Hence the client becomes vulnerable to being misled about what information or service would actually be helpful. And, of course, there is the subtle assumption that there is information available to the client that can be used and understood.

For example, organizations frequently purchase surveys in order to determine how their employees feel about certain issues or even to diagnose their culture. I have argued elsewhere (Schein, 2004) that a concept like culture is not measurable by survey instruments; hence the manager is not acquiring hard data, but opinion disguised as information. When we seek help with aesthetic, ethical, or moral issues, the same caution applies. Experts may be willing to dispense what they deem as "knowledge," but the client must be aware that it may be highly controversial and that two different experts might produce dissimilar results.

The issue then is when in the helping process is it appropriate to be an expert? It would seem that it is most appropriate when the helper's informational expertise is obvious to the potential client. But even in those situations, such as when we ask a native for directions, it is surprising how often we get information that is confusing, complicated, unable to be interpreted, and sometimes even wrong. Or, from the helper's perspective, how often does my effort to give directions lead to the discovery that I, in fact, do not know how to get to where the client really wants to go? I would argue, therefore, that at the very beginning of a helping situation, the expert role is rarely if ever appropriate.

ROLE 2. The Doctor Role: Diagnose and Prescribe

The doctor role is a kind of extension and enlargement of the expert role. Not only does the client assume that the helper will respond by providing information and service, but also expects a diagnosis and a prescription. Again, whether or not clients expect it or ask for it, helpers may choose whether or not to take that role, which gives them even more power.

We are familiar with this role in ordinary life when we go to doctors, counselors, coaches, and repair people of various sorts. Managers often bring in consultants to diagnose and fix certain areas, or have them observe the organization to discover if there are any areas not functioning properly which might need attention. The helper/consultant is brought in to find out what is wrong with which part of the organization and then, like the physician, is expected to recommend a program of therapy or prescribe a remedial measure.

This role puts even more power into the hands of the helper who diagnoses, prescribes, and administers the cure. The client not only abdicates responsibility for making the diagnosis— thereby creating even more dependency on the helper—but assumes, in addition, that an outsider can come into the situation, identify problems, and remedy them. This role is of obvious appeal to helpers because it empowers them and endows them with x-ray vision. Providing expert diagnoses and prescribing remedial courses of action justifies the high fees that helpers can command and makes very visible and concrete the nature of the help they claim to provide. In this relationship, the report, the presentation of findings, the diagnosis, and the recommendations take on special importance in identifying what the helper does. For many consultants this is the essence of what they do, and they feel that they have not done their job until they have made a thorough analysis and diagnosis leading to a specific written recommendation.

As most readers will recognize from their own experiences, this role is fraught with difficulties in spite of its popularity. All of us, as clients, have experienced how irrelevant a helper's advice or recommendations can be or how offensive it can be to be told what to do, even when we have asked for advice. All of us, as helpers, have had the experience, more often than we would care to admit, of having our advice and recommendations accepted with a polite nod only to have it ignored, or worse, have it rejected altogether, implying that we did not really understand the client's situation at all. Clients often become defensive and belittle our suggestions by pointing out key facts we missed or that the recommended course of action has already been tried and has failed. To begin to understand these difficulties one must analyze some of the implicit assumptions of this doctor model.

One of the most obvious difficulties in this role is the assumption that the helper can get accurate diagnostic information. Whether it is an individual or an organizational unit, a client in need of help may be reluctant to reveal the kind of information that is necessary for someone to make an accurate diagnosis. Even in medicine, the doctor has to rely on what the patient recounts as symptoms. Only when a certain level of trust has been built up can the helper count on the client to say what is really going on. Paradoxically, the initial bias can go in either the direction of overstating the problem to get the helper's attention right away or understating it to test the helper's level of interest. In either case, the helper is not likely to get an accurate picture of what may be going on until a trusting relationship has been established.

An equally great difficulty with the doctor role is that the client is likely to be unwilling to believe the diagnosis or to accept the prescription offered by the helper. I suspect that most organizations have drawers full of reports by consultants that are either not understood or not accepted by the client. What is wrong, of course, is that the doctor has not built up a common diagnostic frame of reference with the client and, therefore, may be ignorant of personality traits or cultural forces in the client's environment that would prevent certain kinds of prescriptions from being implemented. If the helper does all the diagnosing while the client waits passively for a prescription, it is predictable that a communication gulf will arise that will make the diagnosis and prescription seem irrelevant, unpalatable, or unable to be implemented.

Even in standard medicine, physicians have increasingly realized that patients do not automatically accept diagnoses nor automatically do what the doctor recommends. One sees this most clearly in the cross-cultural context, where assumptions about illness or what one does about it may differ from culture to culture. But one also sees it increasingly in the treatment of breast cancer where the oncologist has to involve the patient in the crucial choice as to whether to have a radical mastectomy or a program of chemotherapy and/or radiation. Similarly, in plastic surgery the patient's goals and self-image become crucial variables in determining the ultimate success of the operation.

A third difficulty with this role is that in human systems, indeed in all systems, the process of diagnosis is itself an intervention of unknown consequence. Going through a stress test, an MRI, a psychological test, or a lengthy health-oriented interview with a physician's helper influences clients by stimulating their thinking and raising the question of what might be going on in their lives. The test itself may be so frightening that it biases the client away from pursuing the help.

A fourth difficulty with the doctor role is that even if the diagnosis and prescription are valid, the client may not be able to make the changes recommended because of personal or social factors that had not been considered during the diagnostic process.

In summary, the degree to which the doctor model will work will depend on the following:

1. Whether or not the client is motivated to reveal accurate information

2. Whether or not the client accepts and believes the diagnosis and prescription

3. Whether or not the consequences of doing the diagnostic processes are accurately understood and accepted

4. Whether or not the client is able to make the changes that are recommended

5. Whether or not the increased amount of client dependency is a factor in aiding or hindering the ultimate solution

The ultimate problem in deciding when to go into the doctor role is how to know or sense when enough trust has been built up to permit moving into this more powerful position. In turn, that depends upon sensing when the relationship feels equitable to the client, or when the actual power or status differential is perceived by the client to be appropriate and fair. As I noted at the beginning of this chapter, both the helper and the client are ignorant of many things, so to build an effective helping relationship, the helper's first actions must be geared to removing some of this ignorance.

ROLE 3. The Process Consultant Role

Process consultation (Schein, 1969, 1999) means that the helper focuses from the very beginning on the communication process. The content of the client's request cannot be ignored, but the helper can focus primarily on how the interaction is occurring by paying attention to demeanor, tone of voice, setting, body language, and any other cues that would signal degree of anxiety and/or trust. The goal is to equilibrate the status and to create a climate that will permit both client and helper to remove their ignorance. The concept is not to assume too much, but rather to create a situation where not only will the client reveal more, but in that process will begin to gain status and develop trust. What this means behaviorally is to adopt a role of humble inquiry in order to avoid the traps of being seduced by one's initial power position.

Depending on the actual situation, this role may take only a few seconds or minutes as relevant information surfaces about what kind of expertise or doctoring is needed. Or the helper may stay in this role for a long time because the emerging situation requires keeping the client in a very proactive role. In either case, a helping relationship begins to be built because of the interest that the helper conveys through humble inquiry.

At the core of this role is the assumption that clients must be encouraged to remain proactive, in the sense of retaining both the diagnostic and remedial initiative because only they own the problems identified, only they know the true complexity of their situation, and only they know what will work for them in the culture in which they live. Frequently clients may be able to help themselves, and it is often more appropriate to facilitate this form of helping than to tell them what to do or fix things for them. This is illustrated best in those forms of counseling or therapy that emphasize clients getting insight and formulating solutions for themselves. It is easy to see how one needs to be in this role when a client brings up a complex personal or organizational problem.

It is less obvious how this would apply to the straightforward request for information or service. And yet, successful experts and doctors can provide many examples of how they have to be process consultants before their other roles may apply. For example, effective tech consultants or auto mechanics will take a few minutes to discuss with the client what the situation is, what has been tried already, and the client's expectations and fears, before they shift into an expert or doctor role. Oncologists note that before they can prescribe treatment to a woman with breast cancer, they have to build a relationship with her that would enable her to choose what would be best for her. Lawyers may engage in a lengthy period of process consultation before it is clear how the client wants to handle divorce proceedings. Only when a comfortable joint decision has been reached does the lawyer or doctor shift more fully into the expert and pre-scriber role.

I recall a situation where failure to pay attention to the process caused unnecessary pain. A friend who was weak from the flu asked me to help him up from the couch he was sitting on. I grabbed his arm and started to pull him up, only to hear him yell, "Not that one!" because he had a severely bruised shoulder that I did not know about. Had I been more of a process consultant at that moment I would have said, "How can I help?" and my friend would have held out his good arm for a boost.

In summary, the adoption of the process consultant role rests on the following set of assumptions:

1. Clients, whether they are managers, friends, colleagues, students, spouses, children, etc., often do not know what is really wrong and need help in diagnosing what their problems actually are. But only they own and live with the problem.

2. Clients often do not know what kinds of help consultants can give to them; they need guidance to know what kinds of help to seek.

3. Most clients have a constructive intent to improve things, but need help in identifying what to improve and how to improve it.

4. Only clients know what will ultimately work in their situation.

5. Unless clients learn to see problems for themselves and think through their own remedies, they will be less likely to implement the solution and less likely to learn how to fix such problems should they recur.

6. The ultimate function of help is to pass on diagnostic skills and intervene constructively so that clients are more able to continue to improve their situations on their own.

Summary and Conclusion

Someone who is asked for help has a choice of three possible helping roles: expert, doctor, and process consultant. Because both client and helper are initially ignorant of many aspects of what is going on, and because the relationship between them begins unbalanced, starting in the expert or doctor role creates the potential for both the client and the consultant to fall into traps as a result. To build a helping relationship that works therefore requires interventions on the part of the helper that build up the client's status and elicit valid information. Starting out in the process consultant role is the most likely to facilitate status equilibration and to reveal the information necessary to decide on what kind of help is needed and how best to provide it. Only when some level of trust has been established is it possible to get accurate information that allows the shift to the expert or doctor role. As the helping process proceeds, the helper may shift among all three roles many times as the situation demands.

A central proposition of helping can now be stated. Any helping situation must begin with the helper adopting the process consultant role in order to do the following:

1. Remove the ignorance inherent in the situation
2. Lessen the initial status differential
3. Identify what further role may be most suitable to the problem identified

The essence of the process consultant role at the beginning of a helping relationship is to engage in humble inquiry. What this means and how to do it is the subject of the next chapter.

5

Humble Inquiry

The Key to Building and Maintaining the Helping Relationship

The basic answer to the question of how to build and maintain the helping relationship is paradoxical because it is absurdly simple to name and describe, but incredibly difficult to do reliably. At the beginning of any helping relationship, and throughout its life, what is crucial is not the content of the client's problem or the helper's expertise, but the communication process that will enable both to figure out what is actually needed.

The kind of communication process that will most equilibrate the social statuses of client and helper is for the helper to give something of value to the client. It is the client who is initially one down and, therefore vulnerable to being confirmed as indeed being of less value for having a problem. In the U.S. culture it has been observed that this is more of a problem for men than women. In my own experience it has been true that men find it harder to admit publicly that they have a problem, but the feeling of being one down is present in women as well, even though they find it easier to admit the need for help.

It is the helper who must enter this dynamic in a supportive, giving, ego-enhancing way. The first intervention must always be what I am calling humble inquiry, even if the inquiry is merely careful observation and listening in the first few moments of the encounter. The critical point is not to stereotype the situation even if it looks like something familiar. Even in the simplest helping situation of giving someone directions, it is essential that the helper take a moment to think about what the client is actually asking and whether the client's request makes sense. As indicated in the previous chapter, this kind of inquiry can best be described as accessing your ignorance and, because it is genuine inquiry, it is appropriate to call it humble. The helper becomes open to what may be learned through observation and careful listening. The helper's expectations may be incorrect, and it is the helper's willingness to accept new information that elicits trust and makes the client feel better about having a problem. In many organizational projects the client needs to build up self-confidence and realize that help may actually be available.

Let us look at some different kinds of helping situations to illustrate this point. For example, recall the example of someone asking me how to get to Massachusetts Ave. from where I live in West Cambridge. Massachusetts Ave. is a long street that runs parallel to the street on which we were standing, and I certainly did not know where along it the person needed to go. I asked where she was headed and she said she wanted to get into downtown Boston. I was then able to point out that if she stayed on the Parkway that she was already on, she would get directly into Boston, thereby avoiding going way out of her way. Giving her a direct answer would have been less helpful than inquiring where she was headed. It is also possible that she might have been very ill and needed to find a hospital, knowing only that there was one on Massachusetts Ave. Without inquiring there is no way of knowing just what the problem might be.

Consider again the ten-year-old who has just rushed to his father with "Please help me with this homework, Daddy."

Instead of leaping in, the father could say, "What do you have in mind?" or "Tell me more," either of which would invite more conversation, providing the opportunity to reveal what in fact is on the child's mind. Consider, for a moment, the situation of a bedridden post-surgical patient needing the help of a nurse or attendant to position a bedpan when a need arises. How is this to be accomplished without the patient losing self-esteem? The helper must show sensitivity. Before lifting the patient the attendant can inquire, "What would you like me to do?" or "Where is it hurting most?" or "Where do you want me to lift?"

Consider the situation of the computer hotline helper who has a distraught user on the phone complaining of a computer that isn't working. What the helper does not know is whether the user has any knowledge at all, and so must first ask a few questions that determine what the user does know, especially terminology such as cursor, hard drive, and related words that may be routine to the helper but a foreign language to the user. The helper must start with some kind of a general question the answer to which will reveal what the client does or does not understand. Sometimes that inquiry can be simply, "Tell me a bit more," "When did this start?" or "What did you do . . . ?"

Consider the suicide hotline. Presumably the biggest challenge is to get the suicidal person to talk long enough to enable the helper to say some things that will build up the self-esteem of the caller. One of the most intriguing versions of such an inquiry was mentioned to me by a psychotherapist friend who reported that when he has a suicidal patient he asks, "Does *all of you* want to commit suicide? Is there some little part of you that does not want to commit suicide? Let me talk for a few minutes to the part of you that does not want to commit suicide." The goal, clearly, is to make the patient aware that there is a better part, the part that would raise self-esteem.

By asking for further information the helper is doing three important things: 1) building up the client's status by giving him or her the role of knowing something important, 2) conveying interest and emotional commitment to the situation, which encourages the building of a relationship, however temporary it may be, and 3) getting crucial information, which enables the helper to figure out what to do next. From a practical point of view, it is the third purpose—getting further information—that is the most important. Without it the helper often leaps prematurely into the expert or doctor role and makes mistakes by rushing in too soon with advice that turns out to be misunderstood or resented.

Forms of Inquiry

Inquiry is as much an attitude as it is a specific behavior. How it plays out will depend very much on the actual situation. But different kinds of inquiry behavior have different consequences, so would-be helpers must be aware of the choices they have in how they inquire. The helper can be in the process consultant role and still have choices of how to play that role. I have found it very helpful to differentiate four fundamentally different kinds of inquiry:

- pure inquiry
- diagnostic inquiry
- confrontational inquiry
- process-oriented inquiry

Pure Inquiry

The pure inquiry process has several purposes: to build up the client's status and confidence; to create a situation for the client in which it is safe to reveal anxiety, information, and feelings; to gather as much information as possible about the situation; and to involve the client in the process of diagnosis and action planning.

In the informal day-to-day kind of helping situation, pure inquiry may be minimal; but in more formal consulting, counseling, or therapy, it becomes a central feature of the helping relationship from the beginning. Paradoxically, pure inquiry starts with silence. The helper should convey through body language and eye contact a readiness to listen, but need not say anything. The client may be prepared simply to elaborate on the request or start telling the story which will provide information on the client's knowledge, skill, and readiness to be helped. If silence does not elicit further useful information, the helper can choose any of the following prompts as may seem appropriate:

"Go on . . ."

"Tell me more . . ."

"Tell me what is going on . . ."

"How can I help?"

"So . . . ?" (accompanied by an expectant look)

"What brings you here?"

"Can you give me some examples of that?"

"Can you give me some of the details of what went on?"

"When did this last happen?"

"Have you told me everything . . . ?"

"Does anything else occur to you in relation to what you have told me?"

The important point is not to prompt with questions that presuppose a problem, because that is precisely what the client may wish to deny. The questions should always work down the abstraction ladder, seeking more detail and examples rather than abstractions or generalizations. Initially the focus should be merely on what is going on so that the client can structure the contact in a way that feels comfortable. For example, to deal with feeling one down, the client may actually wish to start with an interrogation to test the helper, and say nothing about the situation at hand.

In response to whatever the client begins to report, pure inquiry means the usual attentive head-nodding, the occasional grunt or other acknowledgment that the helper is following the story, and, if needed, further prompts such as "Go on," "Tell me a bit more about that," "What happened next?" and so on. The goal is not to structure how the client tells the story, but to encourage full disclosure, making it possible for the helper to remove ignorance and enhance understanding. Asking for examples is an especially important option because the request for help often comes out at such an abstract level that it is all too easy to project one's own hypotheses about what is going on and miss what the client is really trying to say. The classic version of this is "I wish I were not so shy. Can you help me?" Until the helper has some sense of what the word "shy" means to the client, it is clearly not possible to help. So the helper must ask for some examples.

Inevitably the client's story will slow down or end, and further prompts will not restart the process. In fact, the client may terminate abruptly and ask point blank, "What do you think?" or "What should I do about that?" At that moment the helper must avoid the trap of becoming the instant expert by answering the question. If the helper feels that the client is not ready to hear advice or suggestions, there are several options that keep the client on the hook to reveal more information. One option is to steer the conversation into the next category—diagnostic inquiry.

To summarize, the client's story must be fully revealed, or

else the helper cannot get a realistic sense of what is going on; and pure inquiry must be managed in such a way that the client begins to think diagnostically and in terms of realistic action alternatives.

Diagnostic Inquiry

In this form of inquiry the helper begins to influence the client's mental process by deliberately focusing on issues other than the ones the client chose to report. These kinds of questions do not influence the content of the story, but they focus attention on elements within the story. In the simple example of asking for directions, pure inquiry would be "Where are you trying to get?" whereas diagnostic inquiry would be some version of the following questions: "Why are you going there?" "How have you tried to get there so far?" or "How does it feel to be lost in Boston?" Notice that by influencing the focus of attention, the helper is asserting power and control, which should only be done when the helper consciously intends to move into such a role for valid reasons.

Four different versions of this redirection are available:

Feelings and Reactions. This focuses the client on feelings and reactions in response to the events described or the problems that have been identified.

"How did (do) you feel about that?"

"Did (does) that arouse any reactions in you?"

"What was (is) your emotional reaction to that?"

Notice that as innocent and supportive as these questions might seem, they take control of the situation and force clients to think about something they may not have considered and may not want to consider. Therefore, such questions not only do little to equilibrate the relationship, but they may arouse anxiety in clients who may feel bad about their reactions or may not have any. Asking for feelings may be pushing deeper than the client is willing to go.

Causes and Motives. Asking questions and hypothesizing about causes will focus the clients on their own motivations for seeking help and uncover why things might have happened the way they did in the story.

"How did you get here?" (To the lost driver)

"Why do you think you are having this problem? Why now?"

"Why did you do that?" (After the client has revealed some action)

"Why do you think you reacted that way?" (After the client has revealed a reaction)

These questions clearly force the client to join the helper in figuring out what may be going on and are therefore most crucial when the problem involves other humans and systemic complexity. By asking the client to think about this, the helper is enhancing the client's status and building the client's diagnostic skill.

Actions Taken or Contemplated. This form of inquiry focuses clients on what they and others in the story did, are thinking about doing, or plan to do in the future. If the client has already reported actions, the helper can build on that; but often the story will not reveal past, present, or planned future actions either by the client or others involved in the story.

"How did you get here?"

"What did you (he, she, they) do about that?"

"What have you tried to do so far?"

"What are you going to do next?"

"What did she (he, they) do then?"

Action-oriented questions push clients into thinking about things that they may not have noticed or thought important, or wanted to suppress because they might have been embarrassed about what they or others did or did not do. Such questions also imply that maybe some action was appropriate, and if the client did nothing, this could produce guilt or shame. In that sense these questions also influence the client's mental process and should only be used when the helper is prepared to take charge of that process. These diagnostic categories obviously overlap in any given situation, and they can be explored one at a time or all at once whenever appropriate; but the helper must be aware that any form of these diagnostic questions will change the direction of the client's mental process because they ask the client to examine some events from a new perspective. From a diagnostic point of view this may be desirable, but in terms of status equilibration, it may be destructive because the client loses control and becomes more dependent.

Systemic Questions. Clients' stories typically involve other people—family members, friends, bosses, colleagues and/or subordinates. Stories and problems are usually embedded in human systems. The helper may decide that it is important to know how the client perceives the reactions or actions of other members of the system and may, therefore, ask what family therapists would consider to be systemic or circular questions. If the presented problem involves other people, each of the above questions can be elaborated by asking the client to think about what particular others are feeling, thinking about, or doing in relation to what the client is talking about. For example, in the simple situation of being asked by your spouse for help in choosing clothing for a visit with the boss, the helper can say, "How will your colleagues react to the outfit you are thinking about?" In the complex situation of counseling a manager about how to manage a difficult subordinate, the helper can ask, "If you become more forceful, how will the others in your group react?"

The goal of such questions is to build the client's own diagnostic capacity and to think more clearly about the possible consequences of different remedial actions. Systemic questions thus become especially relevant around suggestions, advice, and prescriptions in that they provide a kind of check on whether what is suggested would work or not. The helper would then add to a suggestion, "Well, here is one thing you could do. How do you think this would work out with the others in your group?" Note that this goes beyond just asking, "How would you feel about doing the following thing?"

These four kinds of diagnostic questions steer the client's mental process and help the client to become more self-aware. However, they are still questions and they do not imply any particular solution. The next category of questions is confrontational because it introduces into the conversation ideas that bear on the actual content of the client's presented problem but may not have been thought of by the client.

Confrontational Inquiry

The essence of confrontational inquiry is that the helper now interjects into the conversation his or her own ideas about the process or content of the story. Instead of merely encouraging the client to elaborate, the helper now makes suggestions or offers options that may not have occurred to the client. Such interventions represent taking on more of an expert or doctor role and must therefore only be used when the helper feels that enough trust and equity in the relationship has been established to make valid communication possible. However, that need not take very long. I have found myself in many situations where I could move into the expert or doctor role almost immediately, either because I already had a relationship with the client or observed an adequate level of trust.

"Did that make you angry?" (This would refer to some key event reported by client. Note that this is more confrontational than "How did that make you feel?" because anger may never have occurred to the client.)

"Did you confront him (her, them) about that?"

"Could you do the following thing?" (Follow with a concrete suggestion.)

"Did it occur to you that you (he, she, they) did that out of anxiety?" (This would be asked when the client has not revealed any awareness of that emotional possibility.)

Whereas the previous inquiry questions only steered clients through their own conceptual and emotional landscapes, the confrontational question introduces new ideas, concepts, hypotheses, options, etc. that clients must now deal with. This may or may not be desirable depending on the helper's assessment of whether the client will feel even more one down as a result of such questions.

Even if the relationship is equilibrated and comfortable for both helper and client, the power of this kind of intervention cannot be overemphasized because it either forces or allows the client to abandon the story originally presented and work within the framework provided by the helper. In this process, the great danger is that any further information relevant to the situation is unlikely to surface because the client is now busy dealing with the new concepts introduced by the helper instead of continuing to share thoughts and memories. The issue with confrontational inquiry, then, is whether, when, and how to do it. This will be covered in more detail later.

Process-Oriented Inquiry

An option that is always on the table is to shift the focus from the client's process or content to a focus on the here and now interaction occurring between client and helper. Just how this might be worded depends very much on the actual situation, but the intent is to make the client conscious that there is an interaction going on, and that it can be analyzed.

"What do you think is happening between us right now?"

"How do you think our conversation is going so far?"

"Are you satisfied that your problem is being addressed?"

"Are we getting anywhere?"

"Are my questions helping you?"

Process-oriented inquiry can also be combined with the other kinds of inquiry. For instance, the question "What is happening here?" is also pure inquiry. Asking "Why did you choose to tell me about the problem in this particular way?" is diagnostic as well as process-oriented. Examples of inquiry that are both confrontational and process-oriented would be: "You seem to want to test me in the way you presented your story," or "I wonder why you are leaving out some critical details about . . ." The power of this kind of inquiry is that it focuses on the relationship itself, which becomes especially important in assessing how the client perceives the helper and how much trust has been established.

Some Criteria for When to Use
Which Type of Inquiry

I have presented the different types of questions in an order that reflects the degree to which the helper wants to engage the client. At one extreme the helper is passive but attentive, giving the client maximum space. At the other extreme clients are forced to examine their own past and present behavior. The risk of offense and either destroying or delaying the helping relationship increases as we go from pure to diagnostic to confrontational to process-oriented interventions. In order to build the client's confidence and demonstrate willingness to be influenced, it is best for the helper to start with pure inquiry and only move to diagnostic or confrontational questions as the client demonstrates in words or actions a level of trust.

If one starts with pure inquiry, information tends to surface quickly and the client is put into a position to recover from the one down position. The steps the helper can take next are then a function of the answers to the following four sets of questions as the interaction continues:

1. How do I feel about the communication process between the client and me? Do I feel reasonably relaxed? Am I getting the story of what is bothering the client?

There is no formal way to answer this question. It is a matter of feelings based on careful observation of the client's behavior, tone of voice, and body language. If I sense that I am not getting the whole story I should be cautious and stay in the pure inquiry mode.

2. How much time do we have? Is it an emergency situation where I should guess at what is needed before I have enough information?

If I feel that time may be an issue, I could ask a process-oriented question such as "Are you under time pressure to solve this problem?" or "Can we postpone thinking of a solution until we have talked more?"

3. What is my relationship with the client?

In a formal relationship where the client assumes that I know what I am doing and have professional training in helping, I would stay in the pure inquiry mode longer. In an informal friendship or with my spouse I would be more prepared to risk a diagnostic, confrontational, or process-oriented question because I could assume that a certain level of trust is already present. If the nature of the relationship is ambiguous, or if the helpers are commercial helpers who may or may not have been trained, pure inquiry would seem to be desirable unless time pressure or the nature of the problem requires instant action.

4. What does my here-and-now diagnostic sense tell me would be the most useful focus for the client right now? Is enough of the story out in a credible way that I should focus the client on some joint diagnostic inquiry? Should I ask the client a confrontational question? Is it time for an interpretation or suggestion for action?

The important issue here is for the helper to have enough self-insight to be able to make a judgment based on what the client has actually said, not on some intuition that the helper might have based on his or her own experience. Often I hear a bit of a client's story, assume that I have been there and know just what is going on, and blurt out some insight or suggestion before I take into account crucial elements that the client has not yet told me about. If I reasonably decide that leaping in with an idea is appropriate, there are two other criteria to consider— constructive opportunism and situational propriety.

Constructive Opportunism

Pure inquiry biases the interaction toward going with the flow, and that must be balanced by constructive opportunism. The major criterion for when to seize an opportunity to shift focus is when the client has said something that has obvious significance to the story and that is vivid enough to be remembered. In other words, a shift in focus or role should be clearly linked to something the client said, not merely to the helper's thoughts or feelings. Especially in deciding when to switch from pure inquiry into the diagnostic or confrontational mode, timing is therefore crucial. Sometimes such a shift is appropriate within the first few minutes; other times one should stay in pure inquiry throughout the interaction. Helpers often jump back and forth among the three modes based on what they hear and how they react to it, but there are no simple criteria for deciding when the timing is right for a shift in focus. If the client does not provide clear information that permits shifting away from pure inquiry, then it is perhaps best to stay in the process consultant role.

On the other hand, one cannot just become a passive inquiry machine. While listening, the helper may have strong feelings and ideas, and they may be highly relevant to helping the client understand the situation. When the timing feels right, the helper can take some risks and seize an opportunity to provide a new insight, a new alternative, a new way of looking at things. In the next chapter, the case of Jim illustrates that seizing such opportunities sometimes results in an error, either in terms of timing or the level of the intervention. The client may then reject the helper, which leads to a period of tension in the relationship. At such times the helper must recognize that the client's reaction reveals not only that the helper may have erred, but also demonstrates how the client reacts to certain kinds of input. In other words, everything that happens is a source of data to be learned from.

We make conversational errors all the time in what we say, how we say it, or in the timing of when we say it. Instead of being discouraged by such errors, we should recognize that they provide opportunities for learning and should therefore be welcomed. We may learn a lesson, such as "Be more careful in how you state things," or "Don't make assumptions—access your ignorance," but we must always go beyond the lesson and ask what this new information reveals about the situation. The learning thus occurs in two domains in that the reaction to the error gives us data about ourselves and what we might have done differently, as well as data about clients — how they think about things and what they are ready for.

Maintaining Situational Propriety

What is an appropriate response for the helper will also vary with the circumstances. Therefore, it is difficult to make rules about how to respond. Sensing and feeling inevitably come into play in assessing the state of the relationship and the situation. However, the helper's intent should always be to build status, or to give face. The helper must get to know the client's areas of vulnerability and sensitivity, and either avoid them or deal with them in a sympathetic manner.

Consider again the hospital patient. One thing that the helper can do is to adopt a demeanor of formality and objectivity by treating the situation as normal rather than unusual. By keeping social distance, the illusion can be maintained that this is not actually happening to a person in real life. Even though the hospital robe often leaves the patient embarrassingly exposed, nurses and orderlies look away and act as if everything is normal. Alternatively, if the nurse sees that the patient is in a very dependent state, he or she may say in a pseudo-parental way, "Let's get you another robe, we don't want you to be exposed out there in the hall."

Another thing that the helper can do is to give positive reinforcement whenever the client does something independently. By saying "good job" to the patient who painfully lifts up his or her leg, the helper is reinforcing the much-needed sense of control that the patient has mostly lost in the situation. What the helper must not do under any circumstances is to show impatience or disgust, no matter how provocative the client's behavior may be. Of course, positive reinforcement must be situationally appropriate, not belittling, as in the case of the computer coach who praised me every time I hit the return key.

In moving from one kind of questioning to another, the helper must be conscious of switching roles from process consultant to expert to doctor. Even though the diagnostic, confrontational, and process-oriented questions are still questions, not assertions or recommendations, they signal that the helper has switched into a different role and is exercising power. Therefore, such a switch should only be made when the helper observes that the relationship has been equilibrated. This is very much a judgment call and presupposes that the helper feels comfortable with the current state of communication and that there is adequate mutual trust to allow a mistake. There is always the possibility that a diagnostic or confrontational question will offend the client. Without a certain level of trust, this can damage the relationship irreparably.

For example, the following incident occurred in a sensitivity training group run for senior managers in the United Kingdom by The Tavistock Institute. During a typical program there were small group meetings led by a trained facilitator, as well as lectures and large group meetings. The approach in the small groups was to minimize structure so that the group could learn from its own behavior. The staff member, usually a trained psychoanalyst or psychologist, observed and occasionally intervened with a question or interpretation. One group was resisting the facilitator's suggestion, which led him to say, "Now the group is trying to castrate me." One member was so outraged by this "psychological mumbo jumbo" that he cancelled his company's future participation in the whole program.

Summary and Conclusions

This chapter has illustrated how some of the problematic dynamics of the helping relationship can be ameliorated by engaging in an active but humble inquiry process that 1) keeps clients in the driver's seat to enable them to regain status by becoming active problem solvers on their own behalf, 2) gives them confidence that they can solve their own dilemma to some degree, and 3) reveals as much data as possible for both the client and helper to work with. Pure inquiry is more than good listening. It involves understanding the social and psychological dynamics involved when someone seeks help and knowing the emotional impact that different kinds of questions have on the client's mental process.

Four levels of inquiry were distinguished: 1) pure inquiry, which concentrates solely on the client's story; 2) diagnostic inquiry, which elicits feelings, causal analysis, and action alternatives; 3) confrontational inquiry, which brings in the helper's own views of what may be going on; and 4) process-oriented inquiry, which focuses the client on the here-and-now interaction with the helper.

The choice of when to engage in which level of inquiry depends on the circumstances, the events in the story as they come out, and, most importantly, the helper's assessment of when the client is no longer feeling one down in the relationship. The actual roles that may emerge for the client and helper will vary with the situation, but the relationship will not achieve equilibrium until the inquiry process has enabled the helper and client to sort out the roles and to demonstrate mutual acceptance. This creates a workable psychological contract between them, which clearly defines the social economics and roles. In the earliest stages, pure inquiry is more relevant because it elicits the expectations of the client and allows the helper to show acceptance and support. Once the client becomes an active problem solver, deeper levels of diagnostic, confrontational, and process-oriented inquiry become possible.

In managing the inquiry process, the timing of interventions is crucial. The helper must balance the client's comfort level with constructive opportunism. In that process the helper will run some risks and inevitably make errors, but such errors should be welcomed as sources of learning about the helper, the situation, and the client's reactions to interventions. Illustrations of how this works out are presented in the next chapter.

Applying the Inquiry Process

In this chapter I provide a variety of cases to illustrate how inquiry works as the key part of the helping process. Each example tries to bring out the social dynamics that are unleashed in various kinds of helping situations and provides concurrent analysis to highlight the lessons learned. Table 6.1 lists the case examples so that the reader can pick and choose in terms of interest.

We begin with a hypothetical case that provides an opportunity to analyze in detail what goes on between two people in an informal setting. The example involves a relatively minor request for help but illustrates the dynamics that develop in all helping requests. In the next two brief examples of formal help I was part of a group in a consultant role and learned how minimal inquiry can have large impacts. The next extended case illustrates the interplay of different forms of inquiry where I was helping a colleague analyze why his helping experiences were not working out. The final two examples illustrate helping a client who is physically debilitated and, therefore, requires a different level of help over a longer period of time.

TABLE 6.1   Illustrative Cases

Case 6.1	Microanalysis of a spouse requesting a cup of tea to illustrate the possible pitfalls in a casual informal relationship
Case 6.2	Helping in a group meeting to illustrate the positive effect of an innocent question (Schein, 1999)
Case 6.3	Helping a group redesign their meetings through providing *process* expertise while staying in an inquiry role (Schein, 1999)
Case 6.4	Helping a colleague to be a better helper to illustrate the complexity of the inquiry process (Schein, 1999)
Case 6.5	Unhelpful help in a hospital discharge, illustrating the negative effects of assumptions
Case 6.6	Intermittent helping in a continuous relationship to illustrate the need for role flexibility and role shifting in caregiving

CASE 6.1: Helping in an informal one-to-one situation

I am comfortably sitting with my wife in front of the fire on a cold winter's night, neither of us speaking. My silence is deliberate, designed to maintain the comfortable equilibrium we have created together. If my wife now stirs and asks if I would get her a cup of tea, she has changed the situation and changed the currency by which we now judge the equilibrium. By asking for something, she has temporarily put herself one down and created a helping situation that must now be dealt with. This is a relatively insignificant request for help, but the same dynamics would be in play if the request had been for advice or comfort.

Following the logic put forth so far, the first thing I should do is to take a moment to consider what is actually being asked for, to adopt an attitude of humble inquiry, to be a process consultant. This sounds cumbersome but is simply a matter of taking a moment to check whether tea is what she actually wants. Maybe it is just an invitation to talk about something heavier. There are several forms of pure inquiry available to me at that moment:

- I could turn toward her with an inquiring look, wait five to ten seconds, and if nothing further was said or implied, treat the request for what it is.
- I could respond by asking her what is going on.
- I might ask, "What kind of tea, or do you want something stronger?"
- I could inquire if she was thirsty.
- I might say, "Should I brew a new pot or use this morning's?"

The point is to create some conversational space to allow new information to surface. If nothing new surfaces, I would, of course, get the tea, which would be followed by a "thank you" on her part. The loop would have closed, and help would have been provided. If it turns out that she wanted something else and was using the tea request as a lead-in, then we proceed down the new path, and my role may shift to expert or doctor depending on what the new situation demands. Such a quick switch is possible because a trusting relationship already exists. Once it was clear that I was paying attention and adopted a helping attitude, I would know how to interpret what she said and could either stay in the process consultant role or choose another. If the client in this situation was a guest whom I did not know very well, I would stay in the process consultant role longer until a trusting relationship had begun to be built.

Possible Problems

Notice that once the tea had been asked for, I could not have remained silent without creating a scene because I would then be communicating either indifference or unwillingness to help. If I stayed quiet, my wife would then have to consider whether I was rejecting the request—which would be painful—or I simply did not hear her. Maybe my eyes were closed and I had fallen asleep. She would instantly look for clues, and if she concluded that I had heard her and was not responding, she would have to try to equilibrate the situation herself.

How could she do this? She could reduce my value in her eyes by thinking that I was being selfish and forget about the tea. Or she could get up in a huff and get the tea herself. This response would increase the value she gives herself because she took appropriate action instead of remaining dependent. In either case, the relationship would be somewhat damaged because the conversational loop had remained open—no help had been delivered and no excuse had been given for not delivering it. The situation was eventually balanced by the client, but at the expense of a minor loss of face and a devaluing of the potential helper. I had not validated her claim to be a person in need of some tea and shown myself to be callous or rude.

I would, of course, be aware that if I remained silent I was threatening her face, and I would also know that if I said or did nothing that I would lose face as well, in showing myself to be uncaring or discourteous. I would therefore know that prolonged silence would not be an appropriate intervention.

So what else could I do and how would those interventions be interpreted?

Let's suppose that on that evening I was very tired and sore from a lot of tennis that afternoon, and that I really did not want to get up to make tea. What are my options if I want to be seen as helpful and still want the relationship to remain intact? What intervention would save face for both of us? I would have to say something that kept intact my identity as a generally helpful person without, however, delivering any help right then and there. I could say, "Let me get it in a couple of minutes," which shows good intentions but also buys some time. Or I could offer an acceptable excuse, "I just need to rest this leg for a couple of minutes." This gives her a chance to withdraw the request because she now has new information.

The important point is that my intervention has acknowledged the request and dealt with it respectfully. I have kept the relationship balanced but have created an open loop for her, in that she now has new information to consider. If she responds with silence, that would signal the possibility that she is offended at my not getting the tea. This would make me tense and would require some further excuse or offer. More likely, she would want to use the new information to get back to a comfortable equilibrium that maintains the relationship by saying something like, "That's OK, we can have it later," "That's OK, I don't really need any tea," or "Sorry, I did not know you were sore, I can get the tea myself." Any of these responses would close the loop and make it possible to recapture the previous comfort. Notice, however, that my failure to just get the cup of tea has left both my wife and me with a memory of some discomfort because of the realization that not every request for help can be counted on to be honored immediately.

Why is it worth deconstructing such a seemingly small matter? It is because the underlying process that is triggered by a request for help is the same whether the stakes are a cup of tea, mental health, or organizational effectiveness. Anyone who is ever asked for help must understand the social dynamics put into play by the request itself. How the would-be helper then intervenes has immediate consequences for the relationship.

In the example above, the inquiry and the process consultation phase might be no more than five seconds. If my wife calls from her desk, "Can you help me get this email out?" the need for me to go into an inquiry mode is the same. However, I may keep this role throughout the whole situation, or I may become the doctor—look over her shoulder, see what needs to be done, do it, get a thank you, and leave. The initial intervention may be the same—some sort of inquiry—but the role that evolves will depend on what the client's response reveals.

CASE 6.2: The Effect of an Innocent Question

Some years ago I was working with the top team of a young company in their weekly Friday afternoon staff meeting. My job was to help them to make the meetings more effective. What I observed was a hardworking group that could never get more than halfway through its agenda of ten or more items in the two hours allotted to the meeting. I tried various interventions aimed at cutting down fruitless arguments, rude interruptions, or diversions to topics not on the agenda, but to no avail. The group always paid attention and thanked me for pointing out their misbehavior, but did not change any of that behavior.

At one point, after I had witnessed many frustrating meetings, I asked in true ignorance where this long agenda came from. I was informed that the president's secretary put it together, but even as the president said this, he and all the rest of us suddenly realized that none of us knew how she constructed it. She was asked to come into the room and revealed that she took items that came in from various executives by phone and put them on the agenda in the order in which they were called in, followed by the leftover items of the previous week. Without my saying another word, the group immediately decided to change the system by having her produce a tentative list of items which the group would then order according to priority, so that the less important items would be tabled or dropped. Both the quality of the meetings and the sense of progress dramatically increased. What had helped the group most was my genuine and innocent question about the origin of the agenda. I had successfully accessed my ignorance.

CASE 6.3: Shifting to Confrontational Inquiry

This same group eventually learned that putting things into a priority order did not solve the problem of overload and frustration over unfinished business. Several members pointed out that the prioritizing process revealed the fact that there were two kinds of items on the agenda—those that needed attention immediately and those that required a longer and deeper discussion, such as long-range policy and strategy. The fire fighting items always had to be done first and lasted the duration of the meeting, never leaving time for the important policy and strategy items. One member suggested that they discuss fire fighting items first each week, but on alternate Fridays tackle one of the important policy/strategy issues. In other words, they could move toward two kinds of meetings instead of always doing the same thing.

This suggestion triggered the doctor in me because I realized that I knew more about meeting technology than they did and they were floundering. I shifted to a confrontational question: "Do you think you will have enough time and energy on a Friday afternoon to tackle some of these tough policy and strategy questions?" This question was partly based on ignorance and partly rhetorical in that I was clearly suggesting that they would *not* have the energy on Friday afternoons, based on my observations of this group. Several members thought that if they took the whole two hours, or even three hours, they could manage it.

I noticed that where they met in the president's conference room, they were still mentally preoccupied with their own work and could not really concentrate or be creative about policy/strategy questions. Based on many interactions over the months, I also felt that they trusted me, so I probed further: "Do you think it would work better if you had your policy/strategy meetings away from the office, free of distractions?"

This was met with immediate agreement and led to further discussion (without further input from me) of a whole new design for monthly off-site meetings. I had, through confrontational inquiry, enlarged the group's horizons around the management of time and space, but the solution of the particular kind of off-site meetings came entirely from them. Over the subsequent months and years a whole tradition of off-site meetings grew up in the company in various departments and geographic divisions without anyone being able to recall how such meetings began. The group had been helped but did not remember in what way.

CASE 6.4: Helping a colleague to be a better helper

A colleague, Jim, asked me to help him figure out why his last four consulting experiences were unsuccessful. His task was to advise managers on how to organize the information function in their companies. His clients recruited him as an expert to provide a specific service. The conversation began with my asking Jim to tell me about these events and prompting him with pure inquiry questions. After about fifteen minutes it became obvious to me that he had been operating with his clients entirely from a doctor/patient model. He felt he had made careful diagnoses and given sound recommendations and, therefore, could not understand how his prescriptions could be so quickly dismissed.

In telling the story he had already revealed many of his reactions, so I did not need to ask about feelings. Feeling frustrated and incompetent, he did not know what to do. The temptation was strong at this point to short-circuit the inquiry process, share my own reaction, and offer my own hypothesis that he may have precipitated his client's defensive responses by his approach. He had been diagnosing their situations and making strongly critical reports to management groups that often involved more than one hierarchical level. He was not aware of the implication of criticizing the boss in front of his subordinates. However, I realized that if I confronted him with my critical reaction I would be doing exactly what he had done—that is, to criticize his behavior to his face. This kind of feedback would reinforce his feeling one down and risk his becoming defensive with me.

I curbed the impulse and instead asked him a diagnostic question: "What is your own theory about why these presentations were not well-received?" In effect I was asking "Why do you suppose this has happened?" focusing on the general events and stimulating him to get involved in diagnosing the situation with me. He quickly identified the possibility that the clients did not want to hear negative things about themselves and that their defensiveness was probably legitimate. But he did not extrapolate to the possibility that his own decisions on what and how to report might have elicited this defensive response. However, his analysis gave us more information on where his blind spots were and began activating him to figure out what might have been happening.

The question of *why* is a powerful intervention because it often focuses clients on things they have taken entirely for granted and gets them to examine them from a new perspective. By choosing the subject matter of the why carefully, the helper can create a quite different mental process leading to quite different insights. A major choice is which aspect will you focus on: 1) why the client did what he or she did, 2) why someone else in the story did what he or she did, or 3) how the event in the story affected the client or others. I thought the best bet was to get Jim thinking diagnostically about his client's reaction, specifically why the CEO seemed to be unhappy with him.

In speculating on why he was getting negative responses, Jim then talked about a particularly painful meeting in which his presentation to the executive team led the CEO to challenge Jim directly. Right in the meeting he accused Jim of overstepping his mandate by pointing out how the corporate culture was not aligned with the long-range goals concerning information. The CEO claimed that at no point had Jim been asked to comment on the culture, a culture with which the CEO identified himself since he was one of the founders of the company. Jim said he felt very bad about this and apologized publicly to the CEO. But, to his surprise, several other members of the team came to his aid and said that his delving into culture and reporting on it was justified and even welcomed.

At this point I decided to focus on exploring further the various actions that had been taken by going to action-oriented questions. This kind of question not only forces further diagnosis, but also reveals more of the client's mental process and viable options for action. I asked Jim why the CEO might have acted the way he did. Surprisingly, Jim could not figure out the CEO's behavior. So I shifted gears and asked Jim why he felt he had to apologize—what had he done wrong? I was, in effect, testing my own hypothesis that Jim should first have given a draft form of the presentation to the CEO in private to gauge how he would react to the criticisms about the culture. The explanation Jim offered reiterated his own sense of guilt from having made a mistake, which led me to try a more confrontational intervention. I asked Jim directly why he had not gone to the president first with his analysis.

Note that with this question I was for the first time revealing my own thoughts about the situation and what might have happened. This pushes the client to think about other elements of the story and is therefore legitimately confrontational. These kinds of confrontations can still be couched in a question such as "Had you thought about meeting the CEO privately to share the culture data?" To keep the client on the hook, the question could provide more than one alternative, such as "Could you have either gone to the CEO or to the group first with a draft of the report?"

The danger of not accessing one's ignorance was revealed in Jim's response to my question. He said with spirit, "I *did* go to the CEO privately and gave him the same material, but I obviously didn't do a good job or get the message across to him." In fact, what had upset Jim was that the CEO had reacted negatively *in public,* whereas he had said nothing in private.

I realized at this point that the form of my question was rhetorical. I was really saying that he should have gone to the CEO and was assuming that he had not done so. This was an error on my part because I assumed that he had not done something instead of simply asking whether or not he had done it. Jim's response revealed my error because he became defensive and again took the blame. But some important new data had surfaced, raising the issue for me of where to go next. I resolved to be more careful in how I questioned someone and reflected on why I had made the error, i.e. time pressure, impatience, and arrogance. At the same time I learned a great deal more about the events of the case and Jim's tendency to blame himself for not having done a perfect job. I also wondered why he had omitted this crucial event in his story and pondered what this told me about his own mental map of what was and was not important. The pattern of self-blame led to a situation where a more confrontational intervention proved to be genuinely helpful.

After Jim reported that he had met with the CEO privately but that the public outburst occurred anyway, I stated a new hypothesis. The problem may have been that the CEO was embarrassed to have the culture criticized in front of his team. Jim responded that this might have been the case, but he had assumed that the executive team was together on this project. (Jim seemed insensitive to the status and power differential between the CEO and the rest of the team.) He also said forcefully that as a consultant, he was obligated to report as clearly and validly as possible what he had found in conducting his interviews, no matter how the audience was constituted. His own sense of professional expertise was seemingly overriding his ability to sense what was going on in his client system.

The lesson so far is that errors will occur, but are there to be learned from. In addition, errors in content must be clearly distinguished from errors of timing and presentation. I might have been correct in sensing that something was going on with the CEO, but I erred in when and how I presented my thoughts. I made it more confrontational than necessary by providing a single hypothesis instead of offering several options.

Sensing Status Equilibrium

As the above conversation progressed I noticed that Jim was becoming more comfortable in speculating with me about what might have been going on. He was beginning to broaden his own thinking about the past events even though he was defensive about the particular issue with the CEO. This signaled that the relationship between us was beginning to be equilibrated, that Jim was feeling less dependent and vulnerable, which made it possible to be more confrontational. Once the helper feels that the relationship is on an even keel, the conversation can evolve into much deeper areas without risking defensiveness because the client is now an active learner and welcomes input. "Even keel" does not necessarily mean that the two parties are literally of equal status. What it means is that the implicit contract between them, the level of dependence, the role of the consultant, and the degree to which the client feels accepted all meet their mutual expectations. Each feels comfortable with what they can give and receive. Each feels that communication between them is accurate.

The signals that this is happening are subtle. Clients become more active in diagnosing their own stories. The tone of voice changes and the content becomes more assertive. Self-blame or blame of others declines and objective analysis increases. A sense of teamwork begins to emerge when the client and helper together figure out what went wrong and what might have been the causes. In my conversation with Jim he began to sound less worried and began to explore more objectively what might have been going on with his four clients. This in turn empowered me to become much more confrontational.

The pattern in Jim's story had reinforced strongly my sense that he was operating as the super expert/doctor/diagnostician and was so caught up in how to do his very best within that role that he had become quite insensitive to process issues. I decided to test his readiness to face this self-defined expert role by going beyond inquiry and giving him some direct and confrontational feedback. I knew that he understood my distinctions among types of consulting roles, so I could be direct.

I said, "In these four instances in which you were rejected, were you really operating as the doctor, giving the patient diagnoses and prescriptions, in a situation that might have required more of a process consultant role? Why did you not share the process issues of what to report and to whom with one or more insiders, even the CEO? Why did you feel that you personally had to make all the decisions about what to report and to whom, and that it had to be in written form with a formal presentation?"

As I launched into this lengthy response I also noticed my own frustration because Jim knows process consultation very well, and I felt he was not using this knowledge. I added, "Why is it that consultants continue to feel that they alone must make all of the process decisions and never share those decisions with insiders in the client system? When we have a problem of how to proceed we should share the problem instead of feeling we must make all the process decisions ourselves." All of this was said because our time was beginning to run out and one of the realities of the situation was that I wanted to get my view across before we had to terminate our meeting.

Jim reacted positively to this outburst and reflected immediately on the question of why he did feel he was acting as a doctor. He was, after all, paid to do the diagnosis, and he wanted to do a good job using his own expertise. But he also had the crucial insight that how he reported, to whom he reported, and in what form the report would be given were options that should have been discussed with some of his confidants in the organization. Jim was now able to differentiate between 1) being the content expert on organization in a company and 2) providing feedback in such a way that it would be accepted and be viewed as helpful. This insight was immediately applied to the other three cases because Jim now recognized how he had masterminded presentations that were perfect in content but had given little thought to how they might fit into the cultural and political processes of the client systems.

We parted with a mutual sense that the hour or so spent on this issue had brought some new insights to both of us. I continued to be puzzled and frustrated, however, about the fact that Jim, who understood process consultation very well, had nevertheless fallen completely into the doctor role and had not seen this for himself nor pulled himself out of it. Though I had provided help, I had not achieved closure for myself.

CASE 6.5: Unhelpful help in a hospital discharge

Recently my wife was in the hospital because a minor surgical procedure had led to a staph infection requiring nine days of intense intravenous antibiotics in the hospital. She had already been weakened by her cancer treatment, so the staph infection debilitated her even more. When she was strong enough to be sent home, she still needed injections of the antibiotic and was told by the discharge coordinator that she could get them in the walk-in outpatient clinic in the hospital by coming in each day. It seemed to my daughter and me that my wife was really not strong enough to come in, wait in the waiting room an unknown length of time, and ward off potential new infections carried by other patients. She had been undergoing chemotherapy, which weakened her immune system generally.

The discharge coordinator explained about the injections and indicated relief that we lived so close to the hospital. However, we had heard on another occasion that this hospital had a system of getting nurses to do home care visits which included giving shots. We asked about this option and the coordinator, without hesitating, said, "Oh, that is *very* expensive, you probably won't want to do that." When we asked how expensive, the coordinator admitted that she did not know exactly but she would find out. Not only did this leave us high and dry, but we were very frustrated that this issue was now being settled on the inappropriate criterion of expense instead of my wife's health and comfort.

What the coordinator had failed to find out was that at this point, fear of further infection and loss of comfort were far more important than money. When the coordinator came back she said with some enthusiasm that the hospital could, in fact, provide home nursing for a couple of days and that actually it was not so expensive. Nevertheless, she continued to frame the issue in terms of expense, raising all kinds of monetary issues around the medicine itself, the IV equipment that would be needed, and the cost of the nursing. The coordinator never noticed the huge relief on my wife's face as she learned that getting the shots at home would be possible.

What had gone wrong was the assumption on the part of the coordinator that expense would drive our decision process to the point that she did not even inform herself of the at-home alternative because she supposed we would not want to pay for something that she believed to be expensive. In the end, the at-home alternative was successfully implemented, but we were frustrated by the circuitous process and offended by the coordinator's handling of the discharge and her initial insensitivity to my wife's health and comfort needs.

CASE 6.6: Intermittent helping in
a continuous relationship

Some of the most common failures regarding help occur in a continuous relationship where both the giving and receiving of help is taken for granted as part of the relationship. This is especially true when circumstances change temporarily, as when someone gets sick. After my wife's staph infection, she set up the procedure for the IV injections at home, but within two days she developed a new infection and had to spend eight more days in the hospital. When she finally came home after the second hospitalization, not only was she very debilitated from the infection and the prior chemotherapy, but she was also warned that for every day in the hospital she would need at least two days of recovery time to regain her strength. So we were in for at least a month of my playing more of a caretaker role than usual. During this time I had occasion to see how fragile the helping relationship can be and how difficult it is to maintain a comfortable, well-equilibrated relationship when one person is more or less chronically in need of help.

One constant in my role was always being available for some form of physical help, as she was basically in bed most of the time. The bedroom was on the second floor, so my regular duties included getting things from the kitchen downstairs. My wife made it clear that she did not want outsiders to come in to help, and I made it clear that exercise was good for me, so I was willing to go up and down a good deal of the time. The most difficult aspect of this role was how to prevent my wife from feeling one down every time she needed something from downstairs. In the early days at home she was also anxious much of the time and requested that I keep her company, which limited my time for some of the chores that had to be done in the house.

One way to help her feel less down was to frequently invite her requests rather than waiting for them. If I was going downstairs anyway, I could ask whether or not she wanted anything from the kitchen. If I was reading the paper I could offer to do it in the bedroom where she was resting. If I indicated up front my willingness to help, she did not have to demean herself by asking. In other words, the generalization can be stated that if the client is in a chronic one down position, the helper must take the initiative of offering help to minimize the client's further loss of self-esteem by having to constantly ask for things. The helper is in de facto control by virtue of being physically more able and must be careful to use that power for mutual benefit.

Related to the issue of being dependent is the client's guilt for having to ask for so many things. The helper can reduce this guilt by providing a self-serving rationale for the helping activities. I kept reminding her whenever I had to go downstairs that this was good exercise for me. If that line ceased to be credible, I would say, "I will get you the glass of water when I next have to go down for my own drink." As she gained strength I observed an increasing number of occasions where my offer was met with "no thank you." I could observe relief in her face that she was beginning to be able to do more for herself. As she became more confident, she clearly also became more comfortable asking for help when she needed it.

Possible Problems—Unwanted Help

What can go wrong in this situation? One time the visiting nurse came to the house to administer some medicine and asked my wife some questions about how she was feeling. I knew she had been having trouble with her stomach, but she did not report this to the nurse, so I intervened and added this to the list of complaints. I sensed immediately that my wife got tense, and

I learned later that she was very angry at my taking over and speaking for her. She did not regard it as the least bit helpful to have me contradict her and describe her complaint in a way that she did not feel it. I had become the doctor without license. She also reminded me that I had done this on two other occasions during visits to her doctor—I had added information that she thought was either irrelevant or inaccurate. Only later did I realize that not only were my interventions not helpful, but it put her further down in her own relationship to her doctor. I realized that it was in her best interests that she learn how to convey herself what she wanted her doctor to know, and that my adding information was actually undermining her relationship with him. I resolved to maintain silence in future visits to the doctor, but satisfied my need for full disclosure by rehearsing with my wife beforehand what she would say. I could inquire and remove my ignorance by asking my wife what she planned to tell the doctor. If she was leaving something out that I thought was significant, I could bring that up privately and we could discuss whether and how this information would be given to the doctor.

What made me a better helper in this situation was my wife's feedback that my interventions had actually been harmful from her point of view. It is a useful reminder that when we are the victims of overhelp, where the helper tells us too much or intervenes at the wrong moment, it is up to us to provide some signal to that effect. Helpers need guidance on when their assistance is no longer necessary, and not much is accomplished if the client says nothing and simply goes away mad.

Possible Problems—Giving up Control

The hardest part of chronic help is giving up the expert/doctor role that has been highly appropriate so much of the time. As my wife's physical condition improved, so did her need to do more for herself. As she became more assertive, she began to participate in tasks that had been my sole prerogative, which required me to let go some of the routines that I had developed and felt good about. I had done most of the shopping, cooking, and food preparation. I had well-oiled systems in the kitchen. I had become expert in these areas and also had developed a certain pace of how I liked to do things. As my wife got better she involved herself more and sometimes worked much more quickly because she got tired and wanted to get the meal over with so that she could rest. I found it very difficult to give up my slower routine even though I still wanted to be helpful in her recovery. It posed quite clearly the need for me to give up something in order to continue to be helpful. I had to refocus on her needs, and her need to become less dependent required me to make adaptations.

As she took on more tasks, she also slowed down some activities such as filling out forms or working on the computer. At those times I had to constantly fight my feeling of impatience. I knew I could do it faster if we did it the old way, with my reading questions and her giving answers, or if I sat at the computer and did the word processing or search myself. I also could not cope with being put into the bystander role of just waiting and watching until she was finished, especially since we shared the computer. I had to learn to make instant switches from helper to bystander to being once again the helper when suddenly I was asked to get something or do something for her.

Perhaps the most difficult of all was to be corrected. As her confidence and energy grew, she pointed out more and more often what she thought I ought to do in the very middle of some of my helping routines that I had become so expert at. Whether this concerned food preparation, driving behavior, or which brand of tuna to get (I had picked out a brand I thought we liked and had forgotten that she always picked a different brand), it was difficult to maintain a helping attitude when my own self-esteem was being challenged.

In all of the above situations, potential difficulties were avoided best through two processes: 1) self-inquiry to gain awareness of what was happening inside me in order to avoid falling into destructive traps, and 2) humble inquiry to get more information from my wife as to why she had brought something up and how important it was to her. In each of the situations I alluded to above, it turned out that once I knew why she was doing what she was doing, I could relax and get back into a helpful process consultation mode. I could let her prepare her own food because it turned out that she had a sense of how much of everything she wanted. I could slow down my driving once I understood that she was still very jumpy being out after so many days in the hospital. I could offer to go back for the other brand of tuna (it turned out that it did not matter to her so we avoided having to go back). I could work on my Sudoku puzzle while she slowly filled out the questionnaire. And as I learned more and changed my behavior, we were able to maintain a comfortable helper/client relationship with my switching role from expert to process consultant as needed.

Summary

In this chapter I illustrated with concrete cases how important it is in all kinds of helping situations to understand the role of inquiry in managing the social economics and proper role taking. In the case of chronic help it is especially important to engage in self-inquiry (to avoid falling into destructive traps) and to learn to switch roles as needed.

8:7

Teamwork as Perpetual Reciprocal Helping

Teamwork and team building are increasingly seen as crucial to organizational performance, whether we are talking about a business, an athletic competition, a family, or just two workers coordinating their efforts. More books are written about team building than any other aspect of organization development. Yet it is still not entirely clear what the essence of teamwork is. One aspect is clearly that every member must perform some role that is relevant to what the group is trying to do. What I have said so far about the complexities of finding one's role in the various scenes of life's theater applies especially when we join a group that is trying to do something collectively. Learning what several people expect of you is far more difficult than learning what one other person expects and needs.

Sustained team performance clearly involves trust that the others will continue to perform their roles over time. Nothing hurts a team more than a member letting down the team by suddenly not showing up or not performing. And social economics come into play as well. As a member of a group, you must feel that what you give is fairly compensated in terms of what you get. Not every member will have the same status, but all members must have some status commensurate with their contributions.

From this point of view one can define an effective team as one in which each member *helps* the others by performing his or her role appropriately so that equity is felt by all and mutual trust remains high even when performance pressures are great. In other words, the essence of teamwork is the development and maintenance of reciprocal helping relationships among all the members.

Two examples come to mind. It is said of great runners in professional football that when they have had a good game, e.g. ran for 100 yards or more, they would take their key linemen out to dinner to communicate to them their awareness that without their help as blockers they could not have made their runs. The other example is a surgical team performing a new, less invasive open-heart procedure in which the surgeon, the anesthetist, and the other members of the team have to be in constant communication with each other and have to totally trust each other's communication.

Amy Edmondson (2001) studied sixteen such surgical teams and found that seven of them were effective and continued to use the procedure, while nine were not able to develop comfort and abandoned its use. What was the difference? The teams that succeeded were launched by surgeons who acknowledged from the outset that they needed help and agreed to joint training with the other members of the team. This allowed them to work out their roles and develop equitable relationships. Key to this was the recognition and public acknowledgment by the surgeons that they really needed the help, which gave a higher status to the other members, thereby motivating them to contribute more to the process. As one surgeon put it, "the ability of the surgeon to allow himself to become a partner, not a dictator, is critical. For example, you really do have to change what you're doing based on a suggestion from someone else on the team.... You still need someone in charge, but it is so different."

The teams that did not succeed began with surgeons who saw themselves as the primary actor, who treated the others on the team as just "skilled support staff" doing their job. These surgeons did not engage in joint training, thereby maintaining their superior status. Without joint training there was no time for mutual role relationships to be worked out prior to performing the surgery. The important lesson here is that teams almost always work better when the higher status person in the group exhibits some humility by active listening; this acknowledges that the others are crucial to good outcomes and creates psychological space for them to develop identities and roles in the group that feel equitable and fair. As the quote above argues, someone is still in charge, but if the group has a chance to evolve, the members can find their niches that both facilitate the accomplishment of the task and satisfy their own personal needs. Status and rank do not become equal, but teammates are comfortable with the appropriate amount of status commensurate with their roles.

How Is Teamwork Achieved?

I am defining *teamwork* as a state of multiple reciprocal helping relationships including all the members of the group that have to work together. Building a team therefore is not just creating one client/helper relationship, but simultaneously building one among all the members. The sensitive team leader is aware that in any new group all new members must work out their relationships with each other and with the formal authority. Time and resources must be devoted to allowing these relationships to be built. Before members can become helpful to each other, the leader must help them deal with four fundamental psychological issues. These must be resolved before their identities in the group can be established and they become comfortable with their roles. As in any helping situation, the leader must function initially as a process consultant and create the conditions for members to gain comfort around these issues:

1. Who am I to be? What is my role in this group?
2. How much control/influence will I have in this group?
3. Will my goals/needs be met in this group?
4. What will be the level of intimacy in this group?

The first question reflects the social reality that we are all capable of being many different things in the various life situations we face. We have a repertory of roles that we draw on when we enter any new situation, and that requires us to make some immediate choices, which creates some tension and anxiety until we know what our roles are. In that regard, the surgeons of the successful groups created roles that highlighted the interdependency of the team members and, through the joint team training, communicated that each member was integral to the process. They selected team members on the basis of the specific skills that would be needed and their ability to work in a team, i.e. to be helpful rather than self-seeking. The surgeons of the groups that did not succeed took on roles that emphasized their own indispensability, which made the rest of the team just hired hands who could be replaced. Team members were selected at random from their relevant specialties and without regard to their ability to function as a team member. To generalize this point, it is status-enhancing to be treated as an indispensable individual contributor rather than a replaceable resource, even if you end up having less status than some other members.

The second question highlights that as humans we always want some degree of influence, but not necessarily the same amount as everyone else in the group. In developing a team, it is therefore critical to provide some time during which members can test the waters—communicating how much influence they need to have and calibrating that against the needs of others. The members come to learn that they have different skills, and that some of them are more critical to group performance than others, but that everyone had some degree of influence on the outcome. This became obvious during the joint training in the successful surgical teams. In the unsuccessful teams, it must have become obvious to the helpers who were recruited that the only integral person was the surgeon, and that they were just there to respond as needed. They must have felt much less important and hence less committed to doing their job perfectly. Furthermore, without the joint training they may never have learned what kind of help the surgeon needed and wanted.

The third question has to do with why we enter groups in the first place. What are our needs and goals and will they be met once we discover what the group is all about? The successful group of surgeons evidently explored this issue before they invited team members into the group. If candidates did not show real interest in becoming a member of the team— because their needs and goals did not mesh with this kind of surgical process—they would not have been invited to begin with. In contrast, the other group of surgeons chose their helpers arbitrarily, possibly collecting members who did not want to be on these teams in the first place but, because of their lower status, would not have had the courage to refuse. In other words, if one is recruiting future helpers, it is essential to engage in a period of inquiry to determine the needs and goals of the people being recruited.

Finally, the fourth question deals with how personally and emotionally involved the member of the group will be. Is it just a matter of doing one's job, or does one have to let one's hair down, by sharing personal goals and information, doing lots of informal stuff with the other members, etc.? We all have our role limits, and when we enter a new group, we have to test those limits to see whether the group will demand too much or maybe not enough from us. In order to do this, we again need some period of training or team building to allow for the possibility that if there is a real mismatch, we can still get out of the situation before the group has to perform.

In the early stages of the group when members are getting acquainted with each other, each of the above questions begins to be answered through the responses that people get. Members experiment with a certain amount of self-revelation and test the degree to which others grant them the value they claim, thus supporting face. Mutual acceptance becomes the currency by which identities are evaluated. Our roles are formed by how much we have to give and what we expect to get out of our membership. Because members have different needs and skills, they may end up with varying degrees of influence or status. The goal is mutual acceptance, which is crucial to the development of the trust that will be necessary to sustain group performance. Mutual acceptance does not necessarily mean mutual liking. Effective teams do not have to be love-ins, but members must know each other well enough as fellow team members to be able to trust them to play their roles in the accomplishment of the group's task.

The leader developing the team must be aware that until members feel comfortable around the four questions, they will be preoccupied and anxious, and will therefore not give full attention to the actual task that is to be performed. If the job is important and complicated, it is essential that the group have enough time for every member to reach a comfort level that will allow full concentration. The effective team cannot tolerate members who are preoccupied with who they are, how much influence they have, whether their needs will be met, and whether or not the group is too formal or informal.

Leaders have to provide time for these questions to resolve themselves, which is why groups often begin with informal activities such as dinners or joint sports activities. This gives them the opportunity to become acquainted prior to having to perform as a team. Groups that fail usually attempt to do their jobs before role relations have been worked out to some degree. Formally assigning roles does not work because members are still preoccupied with the above questions and don't have enough information as to how the others will react to them. This was illustrated by the unsuccessful surgical teams, in which some of the surgeons had the misconception that because the team members were professionals, they could be expected to perform their jobs. They ignored the need to build trust and helping relationships. Mutual acquaintance is a process that requires, in effect, a period of mutual inquiry. Trust and a helping attitude are built out of these encounters.

This testing process should continue into the early trials of performing the task and through performance reviews after the training and practice periods. It is critical for the group to review its early performances for two reasons: 1) to analyze the performance itself and identify what went well and what needs to be improved, and 2) to allow for further role-testing and negotiation. It is therefore crucial in the review process that the formal statuses in the group be minimized so that all members can express whatever role ambiguity or inequity they might be experiencing. When military units do something called "after action reviews," they attempt to create a climate where the enlisted man and the general have equal rights to speak up about what happened and why. Similarly, in reviewing the operation, the technician, the nurse, and the senior surgeon must all feel equally empowered to voice relevant observations, albeit from the vantage points of different roles. This ability to speak up across status lines becomes critical in the operation itself, hence needs to be practiced in the review.

This kind of communication to review progress toward the goal of effective team performance is properly called feedback. Giving and receiving feedback can be viewed as crucial communication in a helping relationship, especially in a group context, and will be discussed in detail later in this chapter.

To summarize, an effective team can be characterized as having members who know their roles and who feel comfortable in those roles because they feel that what they contribute, in the way of performance, and what they get back, in the way of formal and informal rewards, is equitable. In that sense they are helping each other and the team as a whole. Everyone is a client and everyone is a helper, and because they have built the relationships together, everyone can perform as an expert or doctor, as the task performance requires, or as a process consultant, if something unexpected happens that requires some inquiry and improvisation. When the team is functioning well everyone stays in role even though some members may be contributing far more than others. Groups can carry low-contributing members if everyone understands and agrees on their roles. What destroys a team is either that the roles are unclear from the beginning or members have deviated from agreed-upon roles. Such deviation can either be the withholding of help, as when someone does not show up or does not do what is needed, or, alternatively, it can be too much help, as when one intrudes into another's area with unwanted suggestions or actions. For example, when my wife and I teamed up to give a dinner party, we both understood our roles, but I stepped out of role by stirring pots, which made it much harder for her to manage cooking the dish according to the recipe. She provided the appropriate feedback that my actions were not helpful, I stopped meddling, and our teamwork was once again on track. Deviations from agreed-upon roles can also be creatively helpful, as when I turned down the heat under a pan when something was about to burn. In that instance my wife thanked me for the help.

Task Contingencies Define Types of Mutual Help

What defines help in a team situation is the actual task that the team performs and the degree to which the team members are interdependent. On a football team everyone has a specific task such as blocking, running, or getting free to catch a pass; but in more interactive sports, such as hockey, soccer, or basketball, how that task is performed will vary as a function of what others do. What is actually helpful then has a degree of uncertainty attached to it. Team members must not only know how to do their own jobs, but how to react to surprises. When someone handles an unexpected contingency particularly creatively we say, "That was *really* helpful," implying that normal help is taken for granted, but that innovative responses are special and need to be recognized. Because there will always be surprises, it becomes important for a team to review and analyze its performance not only during the trial and learning process but after every period of action. As one of the successful surgical teams put it (Edmondson 2001) "After each case we debrief what could have been done better, what could have changed. And then, that affects the next case." In that review, the behavior of team members should be analyzed in three ways: how well routine performance was carried out, what they did spontaneously in response to surprises, and what turned out not to be helpful. Members can give each other feedback on how they perceived each other's performance.

In the after-action review the more purposeful requests for help can arise. Team members may ask for help on how to do some aspect of their jobs better, or they may offer to help others improve their performance. It is in these interactions that the helping dynamics of equilibration and role clarity continue to come into play. One can well imagine the complexity of the situation if a nurse is coaching a surgeon on how to do some aspect of the surgery better, based on her observation of what the surgeon is doing. Even if the surgeon has asked for help, the nurse would have to be a careful process consultant in the early stages of responding to that request. The cultural requirements of protecting each member's face continue to apply.

During team action the need for help must often be diagnosed immediately and spontaneously. There is often no time to ask for help or to offer it verbally. When the lineman protecting the quarterback sees that someone is rushing and has not been blocked, he does not ask, he just reacts. The operating-room nurse who sees a problem developing in the open incision does not ask what the surgeon wants, but reacts by handing over the right equipment. Such high-level coordination in an effective team does not occur without long periods of training. Mutual trust grows in the same way that it is built up between a therapist and a patient over many hours of therapy. Notice, however, that even in those more trusting relationships, if the rules of deference and demeanor are not observed, or if the help requested or offered is not managed in terms of equity and situational appropriateness, it is easy for the surgeon to offend the nurse or vice-versa.

Task Interdependence

The degree to which a group becomes a team of mutual helpers depends on the actual task interdependence of the members of the group. Helpfulness is most critical in cases of simultaneous interdependence. Two people using a long saw to cut down a tree must help each other or the task does not get done. Six people carrying a coffin can afford to have one or two unhelpful people. A committee deciding on a marketing strategy can get along with mostly unhelpful members. In the surgical team this interdependence was high, so learning how to help each other became a matter of necessity. In team sports such as basketball, soccer, and hockey, the performance is directly correlated with the degree to which members help each other. Teamwork often depends on passing skills and a willingness to set each other up for the final score. Imagine this dramatic example of help on the football field. The quarterback is being chased. The downfield receiver makes a move that gets him free and suddenly provides a last minute target to receive the pass, avoiding a sack. In other words, high performance in simultaneous interdependence is not just an accumulation of individual skills, but the degree to which the individual team members learn to help each other. Team leaders and coaches can enhance that learning.

Where the interdependence is sequential, as in a production line, helpfulness across each link is necessary, as illustrated in a relay race. The person passing the baton appreciates that the next runner is not starting too fast before the baton is passed; and the next runner appreciates the baton being firmly planted in his or her hand. No matter how good any one runner is, if the baton does not get passed, the result is failure. In small teams, lack of helpfulness can be corrected for because it is more visible. When the task is divided into many units, however, lack of helpfulness can become difficult to spot. Take for instance the industrial assembly line or an office environment where a request has to go through many steps to be approved. As customers or quality inspectors at the end of the line, we can see that quality is poor or that getting something done takes too long, but it may not be possible to do anything about it because the weak link in the chain cannot be found easily.

The lower the interdependence, the less important mutual helping becomes. Salesmen operating on individual sales quotas are actually rewarded for not helping each other. However, it often turns out that the presence of large customers who may end up dealing with more than one salesman from the same company creates a degree of interdependence that forces mutual helping. It also often turns out that the independent actors discover that they can all benefit if they help each other. For example, in the famous Chicago improvisation cabaret Second City, two people doing improvisation skits operate on the principle that actor A delivers a line in such a way that actor B follows with the punch line and gets the laugh. The point is that the relative importance of mutual helping depends very much on the nature of the task that the group is performing. Not every group needs to be a team because not every task requires mutual help.

Feedback as an Essential Helping Process

Feedback, by definition, is information that helps one reach goals by showing that the current progress is either on or off target. If it is off target, that feedback automatically triggers corrective action, as when your thermostat starts the heating or air conditioning if the room is too hot or too cold according to your settings. Feedback is essential to the helping process when the client asks how to remain on track. In this sense we are all seeking and using feedback throughout every day of our lives to ensure that what we intend comes to pass. But the information we seek, especially when we explicitly ask for help, is only useful if it is relevant to our target. The helper must be sure what the target is that the client is aiming for, and, therefore, must engage in humble inquiry before offering feedback.

In the group context, getting useful feedback is especially relevant because without it, the group can neither correct off-target behavior nor learn how to be more effective in reaching the target. Identifying progress, reviewing it, and starting conversations among the members that encourage useful feedback—these are all essential to the helping process that creates and sustains teamwork.

Team members have to learn how to analyze and critique their own and each other's task performance without threatening each other's face or humiliating each other. That means that subordinates have to learn how to tell potentially negative things to their superiors, and superiors have to learn how to not punish their subordinates for telling the truth if that truth is inconvenient. That, in turn, requires the ability to give and receive feedback in a constructive manner.

In order for this kind of communication to occur safely, there needs to be a time and place defined as "off line," which permits the group to suspend the usual norms of face and create an atmosphere allowing things to be said that would ordinarily be threatening. The previously mentioned example of Japanese managers drinking with their boss so that things can be said while drunk is one way of doing this. In the Western context, a more typical example would be to structure the after-action review as an event in which the leaders announce that the norms of rank and status are to be minimized, thus setting a more informal tone.

In my consultation with organizational groups or working with fellow academics designing learning experiences, I would often propose a process review, during which team members spoke openly and gave constructive feedback with minimum concern for formal rank or status. This did not occur automatically. We had to learn how to give feedback to each other in a way that was helpful without risking a loss of face. How is this done?

First of all, to be helpful, feedback must conform to some basic rules of interaction defined in this book as essential to the helping relationship. One angry colleague saying to another "LET ME GIVE YOU SOME FEEDBACK!" is clearly doing something other than helping. Even the manager telling his subordinate as part of the annual review and salary discussion, "Here are your weaknesses to be worked on, and here are the reasons why I cannot give you an increase this year . . ." is probably not being helpful. What is wrong?

Feedback is generally not helpful if it is not asked for. As pointed out in previous chapters, the helper must first identify what problem the client is trying to solve before it becomes possible to provide help. When a colleague, boss, friend, or spouse unilaterally decides to give advice or feedback, it is likely that not only will the message be misunderstood, but the other person will be offended and insulted. I have seen this over and over again in performance appraisal where the boss says something like "You need to be more assertive in meetings" and the subordinate has no idea to what the boss is actually referring. That leads to a second principle. Feedback not only needs to be solicited, but it needs to be specific and concrete.

Most performance appraisal systems deal with abstract traits like initiative, ambition, communication skills, social skills, and analytical skills, which mean absolutely nothing independent of concrete behavioral examples. Current efforts to define competencies suffer from the same problem of being too abstract. If feedback is to be helpful, it must occur in the context of a review of action, something the group has done together where specific behavior can be referred to and analyzed. In the surgical team review, if a surgeon says, "I would like to see more initiative from the nurse," the nurse may have no idea what that means. However, the meaning is clear in this observation: "When you saw me struggling with ___ it would have been helpful if you handed me ___ ." Instead of the nurse saying to the surgeon "I wish you would communicate more," more constructive feedback would be "Why did you not tell me that you wanted me to do ___ when ___ ." By referring to specific events that both parties can remember, there is at least a chance of meaningful learning, but note how crucial it is to redefine the norms of deference and demeanor for these things to be said at all and to be heard as constructive instead of punishing.

If we combine these two points, the potential for effective feedback would be even higher if in the after-action review the leader asked members to start with questions about their own performance in order to solicit feedback. The nurse might ask, "Were you satisfied with the way I was handing out the instruments?" or "Is there something I could have done that would have facilitated things more?" By giving the initiative to those seeking feedback, there is a greater likelihood that they can hear it because it relates to something they want help with. It turns the situation explicitly into a helping relationship around common team goals.

Both the surgeon and the nurse share the common goal of

making the operation more successful, effective, timely, safe, or whatever they agree on. Then the analysis, the questions, and the feedback fit into a shared context. For example, it would be pointless for the surgeon to say "You should have done that faster" unless speed was a shared goal.

Finally, a fourth point is that feedback works best if it is descriptive rather than evaluative. The statement "You should have been more aggressive when John challenged you at that meeting" is a judgment. What might be more helpful is "When I saw John challenge you at the meeting, I noticed that you became silent . . ." That opens the door to the client to explain or absorb the implication. It also focuses on what the giver of feedback observed, which might or might not agree with what others observed. By making a judgment on what you should have done, the helper is taking on the expert or doctor role. By making a descriptive observation, the helper stays in the inquiring process consultant role, which allows elaboration and explanation on the client's part.

To summarize thus far, for team members to learn how to become helpers requires situations in which social norms can be temporarily suspended so that they can communicate with each other openly. Such feedback works best if it is solicited rather than imposed, if it is concrete and specific, if it fits into a shared goal context, and if it is descriptive rather than evaluative. Team members who share this kind of communication will develop the mutual helping relationships that will enable them to function smoothly under task pressure.

Though the analysis of feedback requirements was made here in the context of teamwork, the same principles apply to the one-on-one situation between friends, spouses, and formal helper/client relationships. When I think of helping conversations that have gone wrong, in almost every case I discover that what I said was either unsolicited, too general, judgmental, or related to some goal of mine rather that to what the other person was trying to do.

CASE 7.1: Multiple Forms of Helping in the Oncology Clinic

I observed various elements of helping in a team environment when I went with my wife to her weekly chemotherapy treatment at the local hospital's oncology clinic. Keeping her company during the one-hour treatment allowed me to watch the many different ways in which effective help was sought and provided among patients and staff. The staff consisted of a secretary, three oncology nurses who set up the intravenous infusions, a pharmacist who prepared the particular drug to be used, two nurse's aides, and a helper who did odd jobs like bringing patients in who were in a wheelchair. Three doctors made up the oncology/hematology unit and visited each of their patients briefly during the chemotherapy treatment. About twelve patients were usually treated at the same time, sitting in different segments of the unit.

Many years earlier my wife met with her oncologist to discuss her condition based on blood work, CT Scans, X-rays and a physical exam. The oncologist always preceded his recommendations with a great many questions about our lifestyle, travel plans, and attitudes toward different forms of therapy. He indicated that the breast cancer needed treatment but that there were many options available and that my wife had some choices in how to proceed. The effect was to give her value and status in the interaction, which increased her confidence and trust in the doctor.

Keeping the client on the hook by offering choices is a fundamental way of ensuring that the one down feeling of needing help is ameliorated. I noticed that not only the doctor but all the nurses and technicians used various forms of inquiry to gather needed information and to give the patient choices whenever possible. Even the technician drawing blood always asked, "Which arm today?" and "How are you feeling?" before proceeding.

On a treatment day the blood was sent to the hospital lab for analysis because treatment could not proceed unless the counts were within a normal range. The assigned nurse would then come in and talk to my wife about the previous week's treatment, how she was feeling in general, what side effects had been observed and what to do about them, and so on. Different nurses approached this in various ways, but the most helpful method was to maximize open-ended inquiry, by asking "How is it going?" followed by attentive listening. Side effects were often very difficult to articulate, so unless the nurse really took some time to explore, she would not elicit accurate information. Least helpful were nurses who made assumptions about side effects and provided advice on things that had not occurred. For example, my wife never had nausea, one of the expected side effects, but the nurses always talked at length about taking the anti-nausea drug right after the treatment.

While we were waiting we observed multiple areas of coordination and cooperation among the staff—consultations with the secretary around patient schedules, questions about which patient was being handled by which nurse, frequent visits to the computer screens to check on various things, instructions to the pharmacist to get the right drug for treatment, questions to patients about how they were doing, and questions from patients such as "How much longer?" If the treatment cut into the lunch hour, staff members might suggest looking at the hospital menu and offer instructions on how to phone in the order, giving patients yet more choices.

What was striking was the climate of mutual respect, coordination, and commitment to being caring and respectful. Though the patients were, in fact, totally dependent on the doctors and nurses, every effort was made to give the patients opportunities for choices and initiatives, which increased their sense of their own value. I even found it helpful that my wife and I both had choices of what to eat for lunch off a fairly diverse hospital menu. Though there is a hierarchy in the unit that clarifies status and authority among the doctors, nurses, technicians, and helpers, there is clearly mutual respect for what each does, indicated by the communication style and the demeanor of all parties. I rarely heard any orders given. Instead, it was an informal atmosphere of comfortable give and take, much inquiry and listening, and the use of casual humor to lighten the mood. Trusting and helping each other seemed to be taken for granted as the normal routine. Tying it all together was the shared task of delivering the chemotherapy treatment safely and as pleasantly as possible.

When the Team Is Not Colocated

Can trust be developed without face-to-face communication? Can help be delivered electronically, at a distance, to a stranger? We know from various kinds of help lines that some kinds of help are possible at a distance and from strangers. We also know that such efforts to help often fail. The approach suggested in this analysis would then lead to two propositions. First, help at a distance clearly can work if at an earlier time in its history the team has solved the problem of role relations and relative statuses. If the process of team building described above has created trust, the members will know how to interpret each other's electronic contributions or will have the ability to ask what things mean. The desire to help can be conveyed in the willingness to inquire and to respond to inquiries. The kinds of questions asked and their potential impact have just as much relevance by phone or electronically as they do face-to-face. Becoming the expert or doctor prematurely can be just as destructive, or more so, if there is no immediate way to provide the feedback that what is being said is not helpful. So the potential for help is clearly there if the relationships have been built ahead of time.

If the team has never met, a second principle has to be invoked. Norms of mutual acceptance have to be built based on just words. If it is a phone contact there is, of course, tone of voice, timing, and the emotionality that is carried in the higher and lower frequencies of the transmission. If it is an electronic contact, the relationship has to be built with written words alone. In my experience, what counts most here is either the presence or absence of the desire to be helpful. I find that this can be conveyed through the length and tone of written messages. For example, I receive many email requests for help from students and colleagues whom I don't know personally. Sometimes the request is too general and passive: "I have read your book on organizational culture. How do I study culture in my own organization?" or "I am an undergraduate and want to study culture; can you help me?" I find that the same problem I have with face-to-face dependency applies to these requests. I don't really feel like I want to help, so I give brief answers and just suggest some reading.

On the other hand, if the request is both more specific and reflects more initiative on the part of the sender: "I am an undergraduate and, as part of a senior project, I am reading your book and want to use your ten step method in my fraternity . . . do you have any advice for me?" I find myself entering the inquiry mode and would write back, "Tell me a little more about what the purpose of your project is and why you are studying culture." In cases like this I have found that a series of emails back and forth can work very well in enabling me to help this student. Just answering the question without further inquiry usually does not help, as measured by the fact that new questions come back that imply that my answer was not understood.

Unless there is a severe time constraint, a network of strangers can clearly establish helping relationships by engaging in suitable inquiry. The most dramatic example of this kind of network was the Engineering Net produced by Digital Equipment Corporation in the 1960s. Engineers were spread all over the world and most of them did not know each other, yet they built norms that allowed them to go on the network with general requests, such as "Has anyone had a problem like this . . . ? Any ideas?" Helpful responses would come from wherever in the world some ideas or experience existed. The fact that the network consisted of many hundreds of people all over the globe, and that very few knew each other, did not hinder its functioning as a helping organization.

In Summary

What we think of as effective teamwork, collaboration, and cooperation can all be understood best as consistent effective mutual helping. By thinking of these as helping processes, we can define clearly what is needed—an initial informal process of getting acquainted that facilitates mutual inquiry to identify everyone's needs and skills, and to allow for identity formation and role negotiation that establishes relative statuses. Once the group is in operation, it needs periodic review processes that allow learning through feedback and further role negotiation. In this learning process the group needs to assess the nature of its task, the degree (and kind) of interdependence, and the shared goals. To assess progress toward the goals, the group members need to create situations in which the norms of face-to-face interaction can be altered to allow feedback across status and rank lines without damaging the relationships. Such feedback needs to be solicited, specific, descriptive, and goal-related.

To make all of this happen and create a learning situation that will facilitate feedback, humble leadership is required. Just as the helper has to be able to accept help from the client in order to facilitate status equilibration, the group leader has to accept help from the group to sort out statuses and roles. For this process to continue to work, the formal leader and all of the group members must honor the norms of mutual maintenance of face. Claims by each member must be upheld or else the social tension that arises when the norms are violated will inevitably detract from task performance. What we think of as respect or trust is basically the feeling that you will not be humiliated or embarrassed even if your behavior deviates from the norm and is viewed as unhelpful. Instead you will get task-relevant feedback that allows you to figure out how to become more helpful in the group's effort to achieve its goals. It is the role of leadership to ensure that such learning processes take place, as we will see in the next chapter.

8

Helping Leaders and Organizational Clients

Helping in relation to leadership has three aspects. As pointed out in the previous chapter, one of the key roles of leadership is to create the conditions for teamwork where individual members of a group or several groups are interdependent in the performance of organizational tasks. How do leaders create such conditions and how does helping come into play? Secondly, in relation to subordinates, does organizational leadership imply that sometimes subordinates must be helped in performing their tasks? Can and should leaders be helpers? And, thirdly, how does one help leaders? What makes all of these questions complex is that we are now dealing with organizations where not all the people involved are in the room or even in communication with each other. That raises the whole question of who is the client.

Who is the Client?

From the perspective of the helper, a consultant guiding an organization through an organization development process and helping a leader to be more effective are the two most complex helping situations that he or she faces because they involve multiple clients with fixed statuses and roles. Though most of the actual help is one-on-one or in small groups, the client is often seeking to influence other groups or the organization as a whole. The client/leader often wants a diagnosis, a prescription, and sometimes assistance in implementing programs that involve others in the organization who have not been part of the helping process.

Although from the outset helpers know the client's targets for change, the dilemma is that they do not know what the potential impact of the change would be on other parts of the organization. The helper is dealing with an immediate contact client but is making changes for unknown others who have to be thought of as ultimate clients. The helper must consider, therefore, whether the immediate help being provided to the contact client could be harmful to the ultimate client. For example, would the helper want to aid a leader to be more exploitative of subordinates if that is what the client wants? As we will see, much of the complexity of organizational consulting derives from figuring out how to assist a leader in becoming helpful rather than exploitative.

The most common reason that leaders seek consultants is to create the change processes that they need to achieve their goals. And the greatest irony here is that in order to manage others through the change process effectively, leaders must first learn to accept help themselves. They must learn to conceptualize the helping process along the lines described in this book and must become helpers to the organization they are trying to influence. One of the most counterintuitive principles of managed change is that you can't change anyone until you can turn them into a client who is seeking help from you. In other words, for change or influence to really work, leaders must find a way to make their targets into clients. Just as helping is at the core of effective teamwork, so is helping a crucial process in the management of change. In this way, the three elements of how helping and leadership relate to each other described at the beginning of this chapter turn out to be intimately interconnected.

To put this into very concrete terms, an ideal boss would be very clear about the targets that need to be met by the subordinates, but then would be prepared to help them to achieve those targets. The boss would not only provide resources, guidance, feedback, and advice, but other forms of help that subordinates might ask for. The trap for the boss, of course, is that if the subordinate comes to the boss and says, "Can you help me?" all of the problems inherent to giving help apply. The boss needs to be able, at that moment, to be a humble inquirer and process consultant, not an impulsive expert or doctor. What makes all of this more complicated is that the helping is occurring in an organizational context that has cultural norms above and beyond the societal ones about equity and face work. How subordinates ask for help and how leaders provide it have to fit both the broader cultural norms of society and the particular norms of deference and demeanor that operate in the organization.

Culture and Leadership

Leaders are almost always dealing with groups and organizational units that have had time to evolve their own cultures (Schein, 2004). No matter how precisely specified the work is, employees will always evolve ways of doing things that express their own personalities and, where work is interactive, will develop norms and traditions that are particular to that group and the nature of its work. Sometimes those norms and ways of working will also reflect the local realities of how best to get the work done, leading to deviations from how the work is supposed to be done.

This phenomenon has been called practical drift (Snook, 2000) and explains how some disasters occur. For example, in the 1994 shooting down of two UN helicopters in the Iraqi no-fly zone, the fighters patrolling the zone had developed over several years a slightly different set of radio frequencies for their needs, making it impossible for the helicopters to return the fighters' inquiry signals. At the same time, the AWAC patrolling the area was not really looking carefully for a helicopter because they often disappeared into canyons and could not be spotted anyway. Finally, the fighters flew by the questionable helicopters which, because they had extra gas tanks attached, looked more like the enemy helicopters. So the helicopters were shot down with the loss of 26 lives.

The point is that new leaders cannot initiate any change until they understand the norms, traditions, and practical drifts of the group or department that is being taken over. To learn what is actually going on, the leader must become an inquirer to establish helping relationships with the employees and build trust. Groups are notorious in their ability to hide actual practices from visiting bosses; so leaders who really want to change things must involve themselves in the culture of the group, gain enough trust to be told what is going on, and then build mutual helping relationships. The essence of this kind of process is that members work on those elements of the task that are under their control, while building relationships that facilitate those elements of the task that are interactive. The surgeon and the anesthesiologist each work on becoming technically more skilled in their own speciality, and both work on improving their moment-to-moment communication. The sales manager commits to defining new prospects in the territory while the salesman spends time with the individual prospects; they interact around planning how to approach prospects and set reasonable sales targets.

What makes leadership so complex is that it involves both learning to accept help, by becoming genuinely involved in the culture of the group, and how to give help to the group and to individual subordinates as areas of improvement are identified. Helpful leaders must take into account all of the issues of status equilibration and role negotiation. Walking in as the boss and expert will not work.

Accepting Help as a Leadership Function

Many people in senior management positions have the power and the potential to be effective change managers through learning how to help, but their formal position and actual power often lead them into premature fixing. Those at the top of the ladder, in particular, are drawn to the expert and doctor role, whereas effective change management really requires the process consultant role. The dilemma of the organizational consultant is how to get across to clients that they need to learn how to be process consultants and accept the role as a legitimate and necessary part of being an effective leader.

CASE 8.1: A Typical Management Consulting Case

The dynamic complexity of these processes is quickly revealed if we take a typical management consulting case. A senior executive, often the CEO, asks for help from a consultant because a particular department is not producing the kinds of results that are expected and needed. The CEO describes the department and asks the consultant to do interviews or surveys to diagnose what may be going on there and to recommend interventions to fix the problem. The CEO asks the head of the department to cooperate and to provide facilities for interviewing, lists of names, and whatever else the consultant might need. The consultant accepts the assignment and makes contact with the department head to get the lists and do the interviews.

The interviews are conducted over a period of weeks or months and much is learned, but one overarching result is the most troublesome. Many of the managers and employees report that whatever else might be going on in the department, the biggest problem is a perceived conflict between the department head and the CEO who hired the consultant. In fact, many of the managers and employees feel that the CEO is not only mismanaging their department, but is doing a number of things detrimental to the company as a whole. Why is this troublesome? Because the CEO did not ask for personal help in running the company, so the consultant has no real license to give feedback to the CEO. Suddenly the consultant realizes that it is not clear who the real client is and what to do with the accumulated data.

Why not just tell the CEO what was found, including the negative perceptions of the CEO? The odds of that being helpful are very low because it would violate most of the principles of giving unsolicited feedback to someone who does not define him or herself as a client. The CEO hired the consultant to fix the department, not for feedback on his own management style. Most often what then happens is that the CEO listens politely, dismisses the consultant, files the report in the wastebasket and finds another consultant. The CEO learns very little, and is unwittingly failing very important job requirements—to examine his or her own behavior, ask for help, and accept it.

Consultants who understand the helping process as defined here would not accept the initial assignment as given, and would instead begin an inquiry process designed to build a helping relationship with the CEO. The consultant must find out what is really troubling the CEO, why that department is being defined as the problem, why the CEO can't fix the problem, and, most importantly, the CEO's possible role in creating the problem. And all this must be done up front without threatening the face of the CEO. The consultant must suspend the expert/doctor role and become a process consultant until the information surfaces and uncovers what is actually going on and who really needs help.

This inquiry may take fifteen minutes or many hours. The point is not to rush in with expert diagnostic tools before a relationship with the CEO has been established. The reason why this is so important is that the consultant knows that just the interviewing and observing of people in an organization is already a big intervention with unknown consequences. The CEO who proposes to launch such an intervention must understand what the consequences might be both for the department and for the CEO. It must be made clear that evidence might come back that the CEO is, in fact, the problem. He or she must also realize that once people have been interviewed, they will expect the CEO to act on what they have revealed. They will talk to each other, which will change opinions and perceptions in unknown directions, and they will judge senior management on how well they respond to the information that has surfaced.

Helping the CEO to understand all of these consequences puts the consultant/helper into an expert role as well, but it is expertise about dynamic organizational processes, not about the actual problem that may be bothering the CEO. Providing process expertise of this sort is in the same category as when

I pointed out to the overloaded group that they should go off site to do their important strategy work. Such process insights about group and organizational dynamics are legitimate items of information that must not be held back by the helper, yet must be presented in such a way that the client does not feel further down for not having such process expertise. In my own experience the most difficult part of working with organizational clients is how to remain in an inquiry role while providing process expertise and advice. What this means behaviorally is that the helper jumps back and forth between expert and process consultant as the conversation progresses. It is important that the CEO own all of these consequences before the consultant takes any other step. It is the consultant's job as a responsible helper to create a relationship with the CEO that allows all of this to be aired, discussed, and jointly decided on before a next step is taken. If this process works well, the CEO will have moved from a perception that there is a problem department that needs to be fixed to wondering what the best intervention would be to help that department become more effective. With that recognition the CEO will be facing the responsibilities of leadership. He or she will have learned to accept some help from the consultant in defining the problem and will take on the role of being a helper to the department. The CEO and the consultant can then jointly decide whether or not it is a good idea to proceed with the departmental interviews, realizing that together they are not just gathering data, but are launching a major change in that department.

If the joint decision is to go ahead, the next step would be to raise the questions of how this new project would be communicated, how the consultant would be introduced to the department head, and how much freedom would be given to that department head to refuse, accept, or influence the project.

At this point the department head must be made into a client to ensure that whatever information is revealed by the interviews will be seen as helpful to the department. Otherwise department heads could signal to employees to be careful in what they say, thus undermining the openness of communication with the consultant.

In the end, the consultant may end up doing exactly the same interviews with the department. But if the CEO has become involved, the CEO and consultant will have made a plan for how to introduce the consultant to the group, and how to build in some rules and norms for what the consultant will do with the data gathered. A crucial step in this process is the meeting with the department head, who has to accept the role of being both helped and becoming more helpful. That will include consideration of what to do with information that comes back about his or her management style, much of it possibly negative.

If the goal is to create mutual helping processes among the members of the department to improve overall effectiveness, a further issue that should be considered before the interviews are launched is how to surface information and provide feedback in such a way that it can be acted upon. Collecting all the data, summarizing it, and giving summary reports to the department head and the CEO is not an effective way to launch remedial activity around the problems that have been identified. It puts the department head and CEO into the role of fixers, when many of the problems identified can probably be better addressed by the subordinates in the group because they know what will and will not succeed in their work culture.

Instead, the consultant might recommend giving each work unit or team, depending on how the tasks are organized, its own interview results with the instructions to validate the data and sort it into two categories: 1) items which the group itself can repair, and 2) items which must be passed upward to higher levels of management who have the resources and power to fix them. For example, the interactions in the surgical teams among surgeons, anesthetists, and nurses can be processed by them as a group; but if the equipment is insufficient, the lighting in the room needs improvement, or the salaries are not equitable, that information needs to be given to the next level up in the hierarchy.

What this means operationally is that the CEO does not get an overall report of everything brought to light in the interviews, and does not get any information ahead of others in the department. Instead, every group in the department gets its own data first, processes it, and then passes the relevant items up to the department head, who then goes through a similar process of deciding what can be fixed at that level and what needs to be passed up to the CEO. Thus the CEO may not learn what the consultant has found out for weeks or months, but, in the meantime, multiple problem solving processes have been launched which will improve performance. The CEO has begun a process that permits the department to help itself, which avoids the uncomfortable situation of department members being put in the one down position by the CEO looking at the report first and in effect saying, "These are your problems."

As the above processes unfold, relationships with the department head and some employees will develop that allow the CEO greater access to the group, which will provide opportunities to observe and communicate as well as becoming more vulnerable and available. The CEO who then discovers unacceptable work processes or practical drifts is in a better position to launch corrective measures. The key is to develop a climate of mutual helping in the service of greater overall efficiency and effectiveness.

Unfortunately, I have met many CEOs who initially define help as fixing someone else. They want to see the information first, make their own diagnosis (or accept what the consultant's diagnosis is), and then use their authority and power to solve the problems. They use the consultant just to get information without considering that the information-gathering is itself a huge intervention into the system. They do not understand that in most organizations the level of interdependency is high, and that only by creating multiple helping relationships can they improve organizational performance.

To summarize, leaders who want to fix things will be most successful if they initially adopt a helping role which, in turn, requires their willingness to be helped. Once they create a climate of trust, they will elicit the crucial information about what is going on and learn the local cultural rules and norms. They can then move into being experts and doctors in changing what needs to be changed. In the implementation of those changes leaders again have to consider the helping model to ensure that the employees are enabled to make the desired changes.

The Role of Helping in
Implementing Organizational Change

Organizational change is particularly interesting from a helping perspective because in most organizational projects one encounters all the forms of help—one-on-one, team, and organization. Most such projects also include all the forms of client relationships—contact clients with whom the daily work is done, primary clients who ultimately own and pay for the projects and consultation, and ultimate clients who are the ones most influenced by the changes. These kinds of projects also illustrate how change can be facilitated when the goals are initially non-negotiable because they are fixed by outside technological, political, or economic forces. The leader and the consultant become agents of change who have to figure out how to alter the behavior and attitudes of others—the targets of change. One of the truisms is that people don't mind change; they just don't want others to change them. In this truism lies the key—to reframe the change process as a helping process and to turn the change target into a client.

In the earlier parts of this chapter I showed how this process might work with CEOs in launching a change program. Let us examine now how this process works down through the organization if the CEO begins with non-negotiable goals that have been imposed by outside forces or economic necessity. For example, when Con Edison was required by a court order to become more environmentally responsible, employees were required to identify, report, and clean up all environmental spills and other toxic conditions. In order to implement these new rules, the company first had to teach employees how to identify, how to report, and how to clean up environmental violations. Employees could not follow the new rules if they did not have the relevant knowledge and skill. Initially the motivation to follow the new rules was entirely extrinsic—you were punished if you did not do it correctly. But, as employees got more help and became more competent, they gradually internalized the requirements and increasingly asked for help in this area. The more effective supervisors realized that the best way to get compliance was to inquire, "What help do you need to identify and report all spills?" To make this work, the agent of change must convey both the non-negotiability of the goal and the willingness to help achieve it.

In theories of managed change there is a coercive process often called "unfreezing," which creates the motivation to change (Schein, 1999). The organizational goals and task requirements dictate the new behavior that is wanted. But once the motivation is there, based on the realization that change is really necessary, it becomes a learning process, which can appropriately be thought of as being helped to make the necessary changes. The employee now becomes the client, and the agent of change becomes the helper. Framing it in this way is crucial because it then makes the agent of change aware that the most effective way to get the new behavior is to help the client achieve it. That means one must recognize from the outset that the employee will feel one down in not being able to engage in the new behavior without some guidance and training. The helper must first equilibrate the relationship by inquiring what is inhibiting the new behavior, why the old behavior is being clung to, and what first steps the client could take. To get the client to pay attention to what is supposed to be learned, the helper must create an atmosphere of psychological safety and provide role models of the desired behavior.

In his book on medical practice, Gawande (2007) reports on the efforts of one hospital system to get doctors to wash their hands more frequently. After getting only minimal compliance with various kinds of incentives and rules, the doctors were asked, "Why don't you wash your hands more frequently?" This humble inquiry revealed many reasons, such as the inconvenience and time that it took, leading to a variety of solutions that brought compliance to near 100 percent. For example, hand cleansers were installed at multiple convenient locations, which facilitated hand-washing and saved time. The doctors were now being helped instead of coerced.

The Helper Role in Organizational Consulting

As the above example illustrates, the consultant who wants to be more than a passive information gatherer and wants to help the CEO and the organization must accept the ambiguity and complexity of the client concept. Even though the daily work may be one-on-one, the concept of who may be the client will shift in sometimes unexpected ways. I have found myself at various times within a single project working with just the CEO, the department head, individual employees in interviews, groups for joint analysis of the data, or the whole department at a single feedback meeting.

The overarching principle is not to skip levels in the formal or status hierarchy, either upward or downward. If the contact client is the CEO, then the decision as to how to involve the next level down must be shared by the helper and the CEO. Once the helper has established a helping relationship with the head at that level, they jointly must decide how to involve the next level down. Any time a level is skipped, the potential is very high that the members of that level will feel out of the loop, will not understand what is going on, and will wittingly or unwittingly subvert the helping process.

If the contact client is in the middle of the organization, the same logic applies. The helper and the department head must jointly decide how to involve the next one or two levels below and above them and, in particular, make sure that the CEO understands and approves of what is going on. This upward orientation is especially important if the CEO has an I-can-fix-it mentality because many of the mutual helping processes that may be going on at the lower level will look soft and too unstructured to the CEO. I have seen many helpful projects get unilaterally cancelled by CEOs who were not initially involved. In the surgical units previously described, it is easy to imagine a hospital CEO or Chief of Service undermining the adoption of the new techniques due to lack of understanding or a misguided disapproval of the senior cardiac surgeon's "taking time off and spending all that money for training nurses and techs."

In the end, the consultant must realize that the ultimate client is an organizational unit, or the entire organization. For everyone to benefit, the interventions at every level have to be thought through as to their potential help or harm for other levels.

Summary and Conclusions

When the goal is to help an organization, all of the complexities of helping are there. Helpers may not know exactly who their clients are at any given moment, but they should ensure that the top of the organization is involved and never skip a level in building the helping relationship. The way in which work with contact clients will be leveraged into help for others is not always clear, but it is imperative that contact clients must share the decision of how best to involve the next level of client. Furthermore, it is not obvious how one can impose help when the goals have not been set by the client but by some outside force. Yet when one examines successful change programs one always finds that somewhere in the change process there was a critical period where targets became clients. Throughout an organizational change effort, the helper's role shifts back and forth constantly between process consultant and expert/doctor. As the project proceeds, the helper has to function as a process consultant to build a new relationship with each new client. With clients where that relationship has already been built, the helper can play more of an expert/doctor role. The trap is to forget the need to become a process consultant once again when a new client emerges. The helper's understanding of organizational dynamics is a crucial area of expertise that has to be shared throughout the period of relationship building.

A critical aspect of leadership is the ability to accept help and the ability to give help to others in the organization.

Because organizations are sets of sub-cultures, leaders must always accept that nothing will change until they understand the culture of the group in which the behavioral changes are to be made. In that regard they must be able to accept help in deciphering culture. Leaders must also understand that they are part of the organization, and that any changes in the organization will inevitably involve changes in themselves. In that sense they are clients as well as initiators of the change effort.

As leaders interact with others, they must realize that the best way to improve the organization is to create an environment of mutual help and to demonstrate their own helping skills in their dealings with others in the organization. Though it may seem counterintuitive to see one's subordinates as clients who have to be helped to succeed in their job, in fact, this is the most appropriate way to lead an organization. One way to define leadership, then, is to say that it is both a process of setting goals and helping others (subordinates) to achieve those goals.

9

Principles and Tips

Helping is a common yet complex process. It is an attitude, a set of behaviors, a skill, and an essential component of social life. It is the core of what we think of as teamwork and is an essential ingredient of organizational effectiveness. It is one of the most important things that leaders do and it is at the heart of change processes. Yet it often goes wrong. As helpers we often feel that well-meaning help is refused or ignored. As clients we often feel we do not get the help we need, we get the wrong kind of help, we feel overhelped, or, worst of all, we discover too late that we were not aware of some of the best help we got and then feel guilty. To sort out these complexities and to summarize some of the insights provided thus far, I offer in this chapter some final thoughts, some principles, and some tips.

Readiness to Give Help

Though helping is a common social process, it is not the only social process. Our relationships with others have many other functions. In order to offer, give, and receive help effectively, we also need the ability to shift from whatever else we were doing and adopt a readiness to help or be helped. It is part of our social training to be prepared to help and to offer help when the ongoing situation suddenly makes helping an imperative or at least an option. But this impulse to help or seek help can run counter to what else is going on.

We cannot predict when a stranger, friend, or spouse will suddenly ask us for help just when we are preoccupied, distracted, or unwilling to provide help. When students or colleagues come to me outside of office hours with requests for help on their work, I often find myself annoyed that they are not looking up these things themselves, or I may feel threatened because I don't know how to help and am embarrassed to admit it, or I may be preoccupied and unable to concentrate on the other person. Professional helpers are often unwilling to help outside the formal helping situation, as when doctors refuse to give medical advice to friends at a party or when therapists refuse to analyze a dream that a friend has brought to them. Giving directions or advice can be disruptive if we are hurrying to finish something else.

Personal barriers to being helpful surface for all of us at various times, highlighting the fact that readiness to help is in part a choice, not an automatic response, in spite of cultural rules that one should respond to requests for help. If we want to be helpful we must be aware of the internal conflicts that may arise, and that sometimes we may choose not to help.

I find that the clearest examples of such choices occur in my driving behavior. If someone in an adjacent lane uses the directional blinker indicating a desire to get into my lane, I may do one of three things: 1) choose to let that person in by slowing down, 2) choose not to create space by keeping close to the car in front of me, or 3) fail to see the blinker. I find that I maintain an attitude of helpfulness when I am relaxed and not in a rush. I choose not to help when I am in a hurry or will be disadvantaged somehow if I help. For example, I might fear that if I let the car in, it will need to make a left turn at the next light which will leave me stuck behind it and delay me indefinitely.

A similar set of choices exists with respect to beggars and solicitors of various sorts. I can give something, I can listen and decide not to give, or I can walk across the street rather than face the person begging. The important point to recognize is that the need for help is probably around us in various ways all the time, so we do need to make choices about whether or not to perceive it, and whether or not to give help.

Readiness to Receive Help

Readiness to receive help can also be problematic because help is often offered whether or not someone has asked for it. If I am suddenly offered help, I have to react to someone else's initiative and have to cope with my momentary feeling of being one down. Either I suddenly realize that I do need the help that is being offered or, worse, I have to cope with the feeling of being perceived as needing help when, in fact, I think I'm OK and don't need it at all.

We cannot foresee when someone, in order to help, will unexpectedly provide a piece of advice or intervene in some task that we are performing, and we may not be willing or able to accept the help. The most common and often most problematic version of this form of unwanted help occurs in the form of back-seat driving.

To give an example of unwanted help, my daughter was

taking a watercolor painting class and had trouble with a particular rendering of a tree. The instructor helpfully came over, grabbed a brush, and painted in the key lines needed to make it look right, leaving my daughter angry and hurt because she wanted that canvas to be entirely her own work. Sometimes we are overhelped. I was watching a tennis lesson on the court next to me and observed that the instructor corrected every single stroke that the student made, to the point that the students could only be totally confused.

Maintaining a readiness to be helped or to give help means you must inquire internally to recognize when and under what circumstances you are prepared to offer, give, or receive help. This point leads, then, to the first principle.

PRINCIPLE 1: Effective Help Occurs When Both Giver and Receiver Are Ready

TIP # 1.1

Check out your own emotions and intentions before offering, giving, or receiving help.

When our true intentions are something other than providing help, such as getting a job done or beating someone in a game, we are most prone to falling into the traps described throughout this book.

TIP # 1.2

Get acquainted with your own desires to help and be helped.

The cultural rules about reciprocity in the helping relationship are very clear, so if we discover that we don't like to give or receive help, we have to learn to avoid those situations in the first place. Once we are in the situation, we have to obey the cultural rules.

● TIP # 1.3

Don't be offended when your efforts to help are not well received.

Instead of being offended, take a moment to ask yourself whether you fell into one of the many traps discussed in this book. Maybe you did not check whether the person you wanted to help was ready or able to receive help. Maybe you assumed that the person needed help instead of asking.

I remember vividly once trying to help a three-year-old carry an overfull plate of food at a picnic and was harshly warned off by his father with, "Let him do it, he has to learn how to do it himself." Every situation is different, and often help is neither needed nor appropriate.

PRINCIPLE 2: Effective Help Occurs When the Helping Relationship Is Perceived to Be Equitable

● TIP # 2.1

Remember that the person requesting your help may feel uncomfortable, so make sure to ask what the client really wants and how you can best help.

If you have done that, the client will feel a little more in control of the situation and will, therefore, be more able to accept help. Check from time to time whether the client is getting the help that is needed, and be careful not to overhelp by focusing too much on your own need to help instead of the client's need to get help.

● TIP # 2.2

If you are the client, look for opportunities to give the helper feedback on what is and what is not helpful.

Remember that this is a relationship; in your role as client, it is helpful to provide guidance or information so that the helper can indeed be helpful.

The sense of being one down is clear when one has to ask for help. What is more subtle but equally uncomfortable is feeling "put down" by the wrong kind of help or too much help. When someone offers to do something for me that I know I can do for myself, I feel patronized and insulted that the other person would think me incapable of doing it. It also bothers me when I have asked for help and have gotten it, but the helper continues to provide advice. The best example from my own experience as an author is when I ask for general feedback on something I have written. I get the general reaction, understand it, and am ready to fix it, only to discover that my helper has made several further notations and wants to show me and explain every single point. What the helper does not know is that I may have already had the insight to cut the whole section that is now being micro-analyzed. So as a client I also have to learn how to give feedback to my helper when I am not able to receive any more help.

PRINCIPLE 3: Effective Help Occurs When the Helper Is in the Proper Helping Role

● TIP # 3.1

Never assume that you know what specific form of help is needed without checking first.

Even if the person has asked for help or if you see a clear need, ask if that is what is needed before leaping into an expert or doctor role. I have drawn a clear distinction between three possible generic roles: 1) the expert who provides help in the form of specific knowledge or a specific service that the client needs, 2) the doctor who diagnoses the client's situation and provides prescriptions and expert services, and 3) the process consultant who engages the client in a joint inquiry to determine what is actually needed and builds a trusting relationship

that will allow full information to surface. At the beginning of
a helping situation where either you have been asked for help
or have perceived a need for help and are prepared to offer it,
it is best to start in the process-consulting role. Until you have
more information, you don't know whether your expertise or
diagnostic skills are really relevant to the situation. You may
be in the process-consultant role for only a few seconds or for
the entire helping period, but if the help is to be relevant and
appropriate, you must start there.

● TIP # 3.2

In an ongoing helping situation, check periodically whether the
role you are playing is still helpful.

Don't assume that what worked before will continue to work.
The situation may change, so you must be prepared to change
your role. In prolonged helping situations such as teamwork,
caretaking, or organizational change projects, there will be
times when expert services and diagnostic skills will be highly
useful. In that case the helper should switch roles. But to avoid
overhelp or inappropriate help, the helper should be prepared
to switch back into a process-consulting role from time to time
to ensure that the help being provided is still appropriate. Both
the client and helper must become aware that what is suitable
at one point in time is not necessarily appropriate at another
point in time, so both must become flexible.

● TIP # 3.3

If you are the client, don't be afraid to give feedback to the
helper when you no longer feel helped.

I have found that especially with professional helpers or over-
zealous friends it is important to interrupt their often well-
meaning efforts to keep helping well past the time when it was

helpful. The helper has no way of knowing if the client does not tell him when it is time to switch roles.

PRINCIPLE 4: Everything You Say or Do Is an Intervention that Determines the Future of the Relationship

● TIP # 4.1

In your role as helper, evaluate everything you say or do by its potential impact on the relationship.

Communication is not a choice. Everything you do in a situation communicates something and is, therefore, an intervention of some sort. You can be a bystander and pretend not to see or hear a request for help, or pointedly avoid a situation in which help is needed. But even being a bystander has consequences. Others may perceive you as not a helpful person and may not ask for help at a time when you might wish to give it. If you are in an organization in which a readiness to help is part of the culture, you may be viewed as aberrant and be ostracized.

You can see and acknowledge the situation but decide not to act. You can be asked to help and refuse. Either of those responses will prevent a helping relationship from developing or, worse, will be offensive to the client, who may then have a negative perception of you. If you decide to offer help or leap into helping action, that at least will send the message that you are a helpful sort of person. But if you overhelp or help in the wrong way, that may backfire and you may be seen as an unwanted meddler. The point is that no matter what you do or don't do, you are sending signals; you are intervening in the situation and therefore need to be mindful of that reality. Unless you are invisible you cannot help but communicate, so your choice of communication should be based on what kind of intervention you intend.

● TIP # 4.2

If you are the client, you also should be aware that everything
you do sends a message.

Become aware of your own behavior and consider the impact
on the relationship. Are you acknowledging help, appreciating
help, resisting help, or actively denying help? Are you giving
the helper feedback?

● TIP # 4.3

When you are giving feedback, try to be descriptive and minimize judgment.

The issue of maintaining equity in the relationship and ensuring that the client continues to feel OK raises the questions of
when to give feedback and what kind of feedback the helper
should be giving to the client. We know from psychology that
positive reinforcement works well because it channels the
behavior in the direction that the teacher/coach wants it to go.
We know that negative reinforcement or punishment works
well for behavior that should be eliminated. And we know from
feedback theory that the best kind of feedback is descriptive
because the client can then make the evaluation. These are
valid guidelines but they don't solve some of the subtle issues
that can arise in the relationship.

● TIP # 4.4

Minimize inappropriate encouragement.

In building the helping relationship, encouragement—via positive reinforcement—certainly seems appropriate. But if it is not
sensitively handled, such encouragement can quickly become
patronizing and insulting. My computer coach would praise
everything I did, and I found that if he praised an operation that I
had clearly already mastered, I began to feel irritated. I would do
some obvious keystroke and he would say "Excellent!" Inwardly

I groaned. He had good intentions but missed the point that I needed him to recognize: that I was already quite capable of the more basic operations, and only needed rewards for that which represented new learning. The more he commended patently simple procedures, the harder it became for me to fully absorb the new things he was trying to teach me. He was not paying attention to the impact of his rather rote behavior, and I was unable to interrupt him enough to discuss my feelings.

● TIP # 4.5
Minimize inappropriate corrections.

What should the helper do if the client is about to do something or suggests something that the helper knows to be incorrect? The helper's dilemma is whether to point it out immediately (which can be seen as punishing and demeaning), to bring it up later in reviewing the situation, or to let it go altogether. If there are immediate negative consequences, such as when the student driver is about to turn on to a one-way street, it is obvious that the helper should correct immediately. But if, as in learning a new computer operation or new tennis stroke, the mistake is frequent and harmless, the helper should let it go rather than point out the mistake every time. It builds up clients' self-esteem if they can learn to catch their own mistakes. I have also found it useful in this kind of coaching role to ask the client whether he or she wants me to point out errors.

PRINCIPLE 5: Effective Helping Starts with Pure Inquiry

● TIP # 5.1
You must always start with some version of pure inquiry.

No matter how clear the request for help is, pause and reflect for a moment before responding, and then decide in what way to respond.

● TIP # 5.2

No matter how familiar a request for help sounds, try to perceive it as a brand new request that you have never heard before.

Pure inquiry is difficult because it requires you to suspend as much as possible your prejudices, preconceptions, a priori assumptions, and expectations based on past experience. The third person in a row who asks you for directions to Massachusetts Ave. does not necessarily have the same goals as the previous two askers. Each time your child asks you for help with homework, there may be a different reason for asking. The doctor knows that headaches have many distinct causes and therefore need to be treated individually. Every organization development consultant knows that there could many reasons for a client to request a culture audit. And social workers know that all domestic disputes are not alike. Stereotyping the situation increases the risk that no relationship will be built and no help will be given.

The key to pure inquiry is this odd concept of "accessing your ignorance." If you ask questions just to test your preconceptions or hypotheses, the client will sense it and be steered into your domain instead of revealing more of his or her own concerns. To access your ignorance and thereby minimize the bias in the question, you must ask yourself what it is that you truly do not know.

Pure inquiry is most important at the beginning of the relationship for two reasons: it uplifts the client's status and maximizes the valid information available to the helper. The optimum way to begin to build a helping relationship, therefore, is to take the process-consultant role and ask pure inquiry types of questions.

PRINCIPLE 6: It Is the Client Who Owns the Problem

● TIP # 6.1

Be careful not to get too interested in the content of the client's story until you have built the relationship.

One of the most dangerous traps for helpers is content seduction, and this is especially true if the helper happens to be an expert on the matter at hand. This makes it very difficult to remain in the process-consultant role, to focus on pure inquiry, and to access areas of ignorance.

● TIP # 6.2

Keep reminding yourself that no matter how similar a problem is to one that you feel you know all about, it is that other person's problem, not yours.

There is no way that the helper can truly understand how a problem feels to someone else because the other person lives in a different social context and has a different personality. Sympathy and empathy are not enough to warrant telling a person, "I have had the same problem, so here is what you should do." The helper must remember that only the client can, in the end, decide what works best. So the only thing the helper can do is to help the client figure it out.

It is absolutely essential in organizational consulting to keep the client involved in planning the next steps. The helper cannot possibly know the impact of any given intervention. Only the current contact client knows the insider culture and political situation, and so must be involved in the decision of what to do next.

If the client presses you with "What should I do—you have been there," the best way to use your personal experience as a basis for suggestions or advice is to say something like, "I am not in your situation—which only you can assess—but in a similar situation, here is what worked for me . . ." The goal is to present some alternative solutions without inhibiting the client's ability to think innovatively about the situation. The helper should become aware of the difference between "floating alternatives" and "making suggestions." My mentor Richard Beckhard used to say, "If a client insists on getting a recommendation from you, always give him at least two alternatives so that he still has to make choice."

PRINCIPLE 7: You Never Have All the Answers

The older and more experienced I get, the more I leap to the conclusion that I know how to help. It is only when I slow down and pay attention that I realize how often the client or situation produces new dilemmas for which I am not prepared. Because I am in the helper role, it is very tempting to assume that my experience will provide a solution. I fall into the trap of believing that I am omniscient, and then I invent solutions because I feel it is expected. Yet that produces unhelpful help in almost every case. I have learned that sometimes the correct alternative is to "share the problem."

TIP # 7.1
Share your helping problem.

More often than I care to admit I have found that when I was supposed to be helping someone, I suddenly did not know what to do next. When this happens, the best thing to do is to say to the client, "At this point I am stuck—I don't know what to do next to be helpful." This empowers the client and acknowledges the fact that it is the client's problem that is being worked on. Sharing the problem is yet another way to display humble inquiry.

In the rare case where the client snaps back, "Hey Doc, I'm paying YOU for the answers," the helper can then lay out the alternatives and explain why he or she is not sure what to do next. That would provide further education for the client and enhance the helper's credibility.

A Final Word

What I have tried to do in this short book is to reframe many social processes as variations of "helping." These include building trust, cooperation, collaboration, teamwork, leadership, and change management. In doing so, I have come to recognize that helping is at the heart of all social life, whether we are talking about ants, birds, or humans. It would seem then that if we can be more effective as helpers, it will improve life for all of us.

references

Blumer, H. 1971. *Symbolic Interactionism.* Englewood Cliffs, N.J.: Prentice Hall.

Cooley, C. H. 1922. *Human Nature and the Social Order.* New York: Charles Scribner & Sons.

Edmondson, A. C., R. M. Bohmer, and G. P. Pisano. 2001. "Disrupted routines: Team learning and new technology implementation in hospitals." *Administrative Science Quarterly,* 46: 685–716.

Gawande, A. 2007. *Better.* New York: Metropolitan Books.

Goffman, E. 1959. *The Presentation of Self in Everyday Life.* New York: Doubleday Anchor.

———. 1963. *Behavior in Public Places.* New York: Free Press.

———. 1967. *Interaction Ritual.* New York: Pantheon.

Harris, T. A. 1967. *I'm OK, You're OK.* New York: Avon.

Hughes, E. 1958. *Men and Their Work.* Glencoe, Il.: Free Press.

Mead, G. H. 1934. *Mind, Self and Society.* Ed. Charles W. Morris, University of Chicago Press.

Potter, S. 1950. *Gamesmanship.* New York: Henry Holt & Co.

———. 1951. *One-upmanship.* New York: Henry Holt & Co.

Schein, E. H. 1969. *Process Consultation.* Reading, Mass.: Addison-Wesley.

————. 1999. *Process Consultation Revisited.* Englewood Cliffs, N.J.: Prentice-Hall.

————. 2004. *Organizational Culture and Leadership, 3rd ed.* San Francisco: Jossey-Bass.

Snook, S. A. 2000. *Friendly Fire.* Princeton, N.J.: Princeton University Press.

Van Maanen, J. 1979. "The self, the situation and the rules of interpersonal relations" in *Essays in Interpersonal Dynamics,* edited by W. Bennis, J. Van Maanen, E. H. Schein, and F. I. Steele. Homewood, Il.: Dorsey Press.

Yalom, I. 1990. *Love's Executioner.* New York: Harper Perennial.

index

about the author

Ed Schein was educated at the University of Chicago, Stanford University (where he received a master's degree in psychology in 1949), and Harvard University (where he received his Ph.D. in social psychology in 1952). He has taught at the MIT Sloan School of Management since 1956 and was named the Sloan Fellows Professor of Management in 1978. He is currently professor emeritus. He is the author of many articles and books, most recently *Process Consultation Revisited* (1999), *The Corporate Culture Survival Guide* (1999), and *DEC Is Dead: Long Live DEC* (2003). His book *Organizational Culture and Leadership*, 3rd ed. (2004) has defined the field of organizational culture. He has consulted with many organizations in the United States and overseas on organizational culture, organization development, process consultation, and career dynamics. What has distinguished Schein's work is his combination of sociology, anthropology, and social psychology, as illustrated in this book.

Edgar H. Schein, with Peter S. DeLisi,
Paul J. Kampas, and Michael M. Sonduck

DEC Is Dead, Long Live DEC
**The Lasting Legacy
of Digital Equipment Corporation**

Edgar Schein, a high-level consultant to DEC throughout its history, had unparalleled access to the company over the course of
four decades. In a real-life story that reads like a classical tragedy,
he and his coauthors show that the very culture responsible for
DEC's early rise ultimately led to its downfall.

*"A sobering book about the management lessons that can be
derived from DEC's experience."*
   —San Jose Mercury News

Paperback, ISBN 978-1-57675-305-7
PDF ebook, ISBN 978-1-60509-408-3

BK® Berrett–Koehler Publishers, Inc.
San Francisco, *www.bkconnection.com*   **800.929.2929**

Berrett–Koehler
Publishers

Berrett-Koehler is an independent publisher dedicated to an ambitious mission: *Creating a World That Works for All*.

We believe that to truly create a better world, action is needed at all levels—individual, organizational, and societal. At the individual level, our publications help people align their lives with their values and with their aspirations for a better world. At the organizational level, our publications promote progressive leadership and management practices, socially responsible approaches to business, and humane and effective organizations. At the societal level, our publications advance social and economic justice, shared prosperity, sustainability, and new solutions to national and global issues.

A major theme of our publications is "Opening Up New Space." Berrett-Koehler titles challenge conventional thinking, introduce new ideas, and foster positive change. Their common quest is changing the underlying beliefs, mindsets, institutions, and structures that keep generating the same cycles of problems, no matter who our leaders are or what improvement programs we adopt.

We strive to practice what we preach—to operate our publishing company in line with the ideas in our books. At the core of our approach is stewardship, which we define as a deep sense of responsibility to administer the company for the benefit of all of our "stakeholder" groups: authors, customers, employees, investors, service providers, and the communities and environment around us.

We are grateful to the thousands of readers, authors, and other friends of the company who consider themselves to be part of the "BK Community." We hope that you, too, will join us in our mission.

A BK Business Book

This book is part of our BK Business series. BK Business titles pioneer new and progressive leadership and management practices in all types of public, private, and nonprofit organizations. They promote socially responsible approaches to business, innovative organizational change methods, and more humane and effective organizations.

Berrett–Koehler
Publishers

A community dedicated to creating
a world that works for all

Visit Our Website: www.bkconnection.com

Read book excerpts, see author videos and Internet movies, read
our authors' blogs, join discussion groups, download book apps, find
out about the BK Affiliate Network, browse subject-area libraries of
books, get special discounts, and more!

Subscribe to Our Free E-Newsletter, the *BK Communiqué*

Be the first to hear about new publications, special discount offers,
exclusive articles, news about bestsellers, and more! Get on the list
for our free e-newsletter by going to **www.bkconnection.com**.

Get Quantity Discounts

Berrett-Koehler books are available at quantity discounts for orders
of ten or more copies. Please call us toll-free at (800) 929-2929 or
email us at **bkp.orders@aidcvt.com**.

Join the BK Community

BKcommunity.com is a virtual meeting place where people from
around the world can engage with kindred spirits to create a world
that works for all. **BKcommunity.com** members may create their own
profiles, blog, start and participate in forums and discussion groups,
post photos and videos, answer surveys, announce and register for
upcoming events, and chat with others online in real time. Please join
the conversation!